Introduction

Neuro Linguistic Programming, or NLP for short, is a unique approach to personal development, communication skills and psychotherapy recognized in the 1970s. Its approach is to draw connections and parallels between the neurological functions of the brain and the social function of language and the subsequent effect on the way people behave.

Neurology is the "N" in NLP

The first element in Neuro-Linguistic Programming is Neurology. Neurology is a study of the human nervous system, the mind, psychology and the invisible structure or patterns that govern how it all works. Think of the brain for now as very flexible hardware which can be programmed through the senses by experience. But neurology is just a substrate for our experience, like paper is a substrate for ink that writes upon it. Once paper is written on, it is transformed. Neuro-Linguistics and Neuro-Semantics are the experiences, values, beliefs and meanings and identities of life that are written within the body-mind.
Perhaps the most important reason for understanding Neuro-Linguistics and Neuro-Semantics is know how to shape our experience to our will. In some ways, our brain is quite "plastic", meaning that it naturally rewires itself in response to changes in experience, whether we want it to or not. This is how we learn. In other ways, the brain

is quite rigid, reinforcing existing neural pathways that have been born out of habits we have formed. These stubborn habits often have built into them subtle and multi-layered mechanisms to ensure they do not change. In order to change these pathways, we cannot surgically rewire the brain. In NLP, we use language to shake things up neurologically in order to dissolve old undesirable thought patterns and *install* new desirable thought patterns otherwise known as strategies. Instead of using a screwdriver or a scalpel, in NLP we use language as a tool to create an experience that indirectly affects the underlying neurology, and thereby changes it.

The following pages will shed light on what allows NLP to be so effective in shaping neurology.

The Quantum Brain
Computers vs. Brains

Though we often equate our brains with computers, there are vast differences in structure, function, and *capability*. There really is no comparison.

Computers did not evolve on their own. They are not driven to exist. Just like any other tool since our beginnings, computers were designed by humans as tools to give us an advantage in present and future circumstances. If our lives depended on computers to maintain our physical functions, we would not be here. For the vicissitudes of life, computers are yet quite ill-adapted.

While computers are very efficient and very reliable at working computations where the inputs lead to outputs based on certain rules or heuristics, they are not very good at looking at unfamiliar situations, and coming up with new explanations, or rewriting their own programming to cope with external change.

Brains are a Quantum Mechanical Device

Our neurology (including our brain) is a holographic substrate created from the stuff of the physical universe, yet organized to interact with that universe at the quantum level. On this marvelous holographic substrate is scribed information about the universe, which is organized and reflected back at the universe in billions of neural firings every second.

Our neurological system originated from the same stem cells that created our skin, eyes, ears, noses and tongues. The outer sensory organs are originally extensions of the brain, and the mind-body energized by emotions forms a complete cybernetic system, capable of surviving and re-producing in the world.

Our brains were shaped by eons of evolution, in a world where the problems of survival as individuals, as a species, and later as cultures were and continue to be a constant sculpting force. Survive and propagate, or die. In this setting, the brain emerged as a superb recognizer and generator of patterns in the realms of space and time, and energy and material use. To survive and propagate, our brains operate at, and shift between and among many complex levels of abstraction, which invent and reinvent themselves as the *environment* changes.

We are perceivers in a quantum universe... cartographers on a journey to survey and map out this strange universe. The more we map it, the stranger it gets.

What is the Mind?

In NLP, we know that "mind" is an artificial construct. The mind is just an idea, a name, a label, a *nominalization* we give to that part of our selves that is self-aware, and infinitely reflexive, constantly seeking to frame what it perceives, and give it meaning relative to our self awareness.

We all have a mind, and in NLP we know that a mind is something that can be changed, even sometimes lost. Nobody has ever seen a mind. You cannot put a mind in a wheelbarrow. The evidence for the mind's existence at all is based on indirect or subjective evidence. We assume it exists as an a priori category.

In NLP, we look at the mind as the structure of subjective experience, and to plumb the depths of that structure and experience itself, we need some models that can be tested:

We can begin by exploring and charting our minds as individuals:

- *Conscious* Mind
- *Unconscious* Mind
- How we Learn

Then we can explore our collective human mind in several fruitful ways:

- *Neurological Levels*
- The Hero's Journey
- Spiral Dynamics
- Social Intelligence

Throughout this exploration, remember that we are just presenting models, or abstract ways of looking at our subjective mind, in order to provide some understanding or predictive *value*. But as always, remember that these models are not reality, only various faceted reflections of reality as we experience it.

Conscious Mind
The Impossible Definition of Consciousness
We all have a conscious mind, but we zig and zag, and spin in circles trying to define it. Go ahead and try to define consciousness for a buddy, and watch the strange look on his or her face!

For centuries, philosophers, physicists, psychologists, psychiatrists, religions, governments have tried to come up with a definition of consciousness, and have failed to produce a definition that everyone can agree to. Some believe consciousness is a result of mental machinery that could be understood if we just understood the machinery better. Some believe it is a gift of God, and fear to tread there.

We know that we lose consciousness every time we go to sleep, and gain it when we wake up, but we don't know how or why it works.

The Working NLP Definition of Consciousness
In NLP, the working definition of the conscious mind is this:

Whatever we are aware of in the present moment.

This simple definition gives us something we can actually work with, since we are interested in directing the mind toward outcomes that we want, and away from outcomes that we do not want.

Mindfulness
Mindfulness is a practice observed formally in Zen Buddhism and other *spiritual* centers, but a mindful lifestyle is being adopted by increasing numbers of people everywhere. The only way to "know thyself"

is by becoming familiar with what goes on inside that mind of yours.

Meditation is a great way to understand your mind through direct contact with it. NLP is another way of approaching the mind directly. By observing your own thoughts and coming to know your mind intimately, you create the conditions for powerful and intentional change.

Deletions, Distortions and Generalizations
How We Encode Experience

As we take experience in from the outside world, our neurology encodes that experience into memories, but very much *unlike* a tape recorder. Rather than store the information sequentially, we store it semantically. We remember the gist or the meaning of an experience.

Our *unconscious* mind takes in information at the estimate rate of 40 million bits per second (things like temperature, place in space, balance, sights, sounds, smells, tastes, textures, pressure, etc. However, our conscous mind can only process about 40 bits of this information per second. We are wired to only pay attention to things that are remarkable in our *environment*, such as danger or threats, or opportunities for food, sex, pleasure, etc. Most of us can only hold 3 to 7 facts in our conscious mind at any one time.

Because of the way our neurology is organized, we are extremely good at pattern recognition and reactions, but we are not as good as we might think at being logical. Most of the time, we use heuristics (a fancy word for rules of thumb) to get through each moment of every day.

NLP recognizes that in our subjective experiences,

we tend to filter most of reality to reinforce what we already believe about the world.

Deletion

Deletion is the process of leaving bits of information out. We omit and conveniently forget information, especially when in is unremarkable, or when it conflicts with an existing frame of reference. All this deleting is born of a survival mechanism that budgets precious attention to those things that will help us live longer, live safer, live better, or have more.

Deleting is the inverse of sorting. We sort through a haystack to find a needle. We sort through the internet every time we google a term. We delete things that are not of interest to us, again because attention is limited, and precious.

Our physiological states directly influence what we sort for. For example, when we are hungry or thirsty, we sort through our map of the world for refreshment. When our thirst is slaked, we sort through our maps of the world for resources to support the task at hand. When in the mood for love, we go stupid filtering out anything that does not lead to satisfaction. When we smell smoke, we sort through our maps for the nearest exit.

Deletions also show up in our speech and writing as:
- Simple Deletions
- Comparisons
- *Unspecified Verbs*
- Unspecified Referential Indices
- Lost Perfomatives

Distortion

Distortion is transforming or interpreting information in someway before making it part of our map.

Have you ever seen a dark spot moving across the floor and felt a feeling of panic while you thought it was a spider? Later when you discovered the spot was a piece of lint blowing across the floor you felt very differently about it.

Distortion also reveals itself as in our communication as:
- *Presuppositions*
- Cause-Effect
- Mind Reads
- Nominalizations
- Complex Equivalences
- The Verb "To Be"

Generalization

Generalization is a brilliant process that allows us to categorize the world in terms of how things are like or different from other things. We group, lump, classify, categorize all the time. Generalizing is an important aspect of learning and sharing information that helps us operated very efficiently in the world. When we learn a new skill and can apply that skill to new contexts, then we have generalization to thank.

But there is also a dark side to generalization. When we generalize everything as positive, it is possible to accept poison with the potion. When we generalize everything as negative, we miss out on great opportunities. We lack the ability to distinguish. When you see the world through the eyes of a hammer, then everything looks like a nail. We learn best when we remain flexible in our generalizations, and updating our categories as more experience is gained and finer distinctions are made, rather than holding tightly to the first impression.

Generalizations can also be heard in our communications as:
- Universals

Modal Operators

Eliciting Submodalities
What's it like in there?

Eliciting Submomalities is the NLP term for learning how we represent the outside world in our internal maps. We already know how to do this to some degree, and every time we ask somebody to recount an experience, we are doing it. In NLP, we just want to do it more skillfully and with *positive intention*.

Remember that *submodalities* are the way we structure our experience. Submodalities are the components of experience consisting of sights, sounds, smells, tastes, touches.

In order to help bring the building blocks of experience into the awareness of yourself or a client so that they can be manipulated, the skill of eliciting submodalities is required.

The common aspects to all experience are:
- What is the perceived location of the experience?
- What is the perceived distance of the experience?
- What is the intensity of the experience?
- Was the experience associated or dissociated?

So in addition to simply asking someone to recount their experience, we ask additional questions about how the experience was represented, so that when we present it back to the person, we present it in a way that seems like how they perceived it.

Submodalities **are the Interface between God and Our Experience of God.**

NLP opened my eyes to an important aspect of how the mundane temporal and spiritual timeless worlds would communicate.

In NLP we ask "how do you know that", or "how do you do that"? The how reveals a lot about how experience of things outside are laid down on the inside. All experience is sensory, and all sensory experience can be described by their submodalities, and those submodalities differ from person to person. From there, we add cultural and personal meaning to the actual neurological experience as it was recorded.

In this discussion, we are not interested in a philosophical discussion about what God is or is not (which is metaphorical or symbolic). We are not interested in defining God. We are more interested in how God is experienced directly, in sensory terms, and in exploring our own experiences in those same sensory terms.

Let's start with a reminder of the sensory modes: Seeing, Hearing, Feeling, Tasting and Smelling. Each of these sensory modes has qualitative aspects to them, called submodalities, which are scribed in our neurology. From there our direct sensory experience is imbued with meaning from prior experience.

Now, Let's examine the submodalities of our experience of God, one sense mode at a time.

Submodalities of Seeing

It's difficult to find anyone alive today who could tell you what God looks like from their own experience. Though there are religions that stand by the holy word that God spoke face-to-face to some prophet or another, no contemporary religious leader could defend his or her own visions publicly. The fewer the details, the more credible they are. Specificity is a place they cannot go. Various forms of God are depicted in art, but nobody can agree on whether God is more or less than 6 feet tall, parts his or her hair on the left or right, or has any other distinct physical characteristics. God is powerful, if not photogenic.

So from our respective cultures, we absorb what data is available to us. We rely on art and sacred stories to sketch a conceptual model of what God might look like, and we fill in the details. To a white child raised in the West, God is a white male, and to a black child God is a black male. On the other side of the globe, God is more likely to be pictured as imminent, or present in all things.

Are these images reliable? Maybe empirically no, but they are salient and pervasive to the subjective mind, and form an important part of our *identity*, our worth and *value* in the world, and our privileges and direction through life.

Explore your own images of God. Do you see God a person? If so, is God male or female, or both somehow? Does God have a glow? What is God wearing? Is God moving, or still like a photograph? How big is God? Are there boundaries or edges to God's being? How near or far? Does God resemble an image you've seen somewhere before? When you focus your vision on your image of God, what happens? Does it get clearer, or fuzzier?

Submodalities of Hearing

Holy books announce that God has spoken in times past to or through prophets, saints, sages, gurus, wise men, scientists, philosophers, bodhisattvas, and his words have been written, and often translated for us. To the degree that we do or don't believe those accounts depends on how that voice resounds in our inner ear, and whether that voice then is a motivating force.

People who might hear God's voice in the present day as often report that there is no sound as that there is. Some say that God's voice is silence. For those who do hear his voice, there are certain submodalities, which again cannot be agreed on empirically, but which are subjectively substantive. Explore your own perceptions of God's voice, or if you have difficulty, what would it sound like if you could hear it? How would you recognize it as God's voice? What is the tone? How loud is it? Does it have a certain timbre or instrumental quality? How quickly does God speak? What direction does the voice come from? How far away is it? What other possible effects such as reverb or echo are there? What language does God speak to you? Is there an accent? What is the choice of the words? When you listen even more to that voice, is it your own voice? Is it very similar to someone else's? Whose? As you tune your ear even more to the sound of the voice, does it get clearer or harder to make out?

Submodalities of Feeling

Some people feel God intensely, and others cannot feel God at all. Whether one can or cannot feel God's presence is strongly correlated with one's *belief* in God.

Feelings are never "out there", they are always "in here"... always subjective. Feelings can be talked about, sung about, but they cannot be pointed to, weighed or measured. We may think we are sharing feelings, but what we are really doing is empathizing, reflecting or mirroring on the inside. Explore your feelings of God. Where is that feeling? Is the feeling on the skin, or in the viscera? Where does it start and end? How does it move through you? Where does the feeling seem enter and exit, or start and end? How long does it last? Does it have weight or lightness to it? Does it spin, twist or rotate? Is the feeling warm or cool? What places or situations are conducive to that feeling? Do other people or literature tend to bring that feeling on? Are those feelings anchored to anything that might be deliberately controlled by someone other than God?

Submodalities of Taste and Smell

Though Eastern religions have use "one taste" as a metaphor for God or Spirit, there is not much literature, art, or discussion on the taste and smell of God. One would have to be very close to God indeed to have tasted or whiffed. Intimate contact would have to be made. This cannot be done from any distance at all.

Explore whether you have any kind of taste or smell of God as you hold God in mind. Is the lack of any experience due to your own distance from God as you perceive, or might there also be a complete cultural vacuum where the taste of God is unknowable, let alone something to be celebrated.

Location in Space and Time

Finally, we enter the dimensions of Space and Time. Sight and Sound are our best senses for knowing where we and others are in space, and our feelings can tell us whether we are in the present moment or carried by our thoughts into memories of the past or possibilities of the future. Explore where you position God in space and time. Does God have an address? Can you point to the direction where God is? How far or near? How much space does God inhabit? Is God up, or down? As the world rotates, where is God relative to your position? Does God cast a shadow? Is God around you, or within you, or some combination at one time or another?

Now let's explore your *timeline*. Is God a figure from the past? Is God available in the present? Will there be a meeting between you and God in the future? If so, what lies beyond that meeting? Does God's form change as you compare past, present and future?

Practical Application

I am still trying to discover a common ground for understanding our cultural and personal differences. With the understanding that submodalities offers, we can be catalysts for positive influence on ourselves and others. Change the submodalities, change the experience. Change the experience, change the map. Change the map, change the territory. There are as many paths to experiencing or denying God directly as there are people. Whether faith, devotion, agnosticism, or atheism is your creed, understanding direct experience can offer a bridge from where you have been to where you want to be.

In other words, if you change the way you speak, it will have knock on effects in terms of the way you think and behave. Likewise, a change of thought patterns will manifest itself in a changed means of expression through language, and in a person's social behavior.

In short, NLP offers individuals an extremely powerful tool to effectively change thought patterns, negative behaviors' and social problems, simply by concentrating on their words, thoughts and body language! Many books have been written on the in-depth functions of NLP; and many practitioners make a handsome living out of providing therapy and self-help courses. The simple fact is that you do not have to understand the physiological processes behind NLP in order to take advantage of its empowering truths. This article introduces five basic techniques that allow you to harness the power of NLP to change your life today.

1. RAPPORT

The art of rapport is perhaps the most accessible of NLP techniques and beyond doubt the most important in terms of how it will affect your life. Rapport is the means by which you can empathize with and get on with other people; and is a blend of tact, body language and listening.

A person who is instinctively able to build rapport with their fellow human beings will be more likely to be happy at home and at work, to have more friends, be more healthy and live longer. The good news is that building rapport is not a matter of chance. There are a number of methods that can enable you to improve your relationships with others; which are accessible to anyone and everyone!

I briefly introduced the five basic 'planks' of NLP, which together constitute a powerful arsenal for anyone serious about improving their mental wellbeing. The easiest and most accessible of these NLP techniques involves improving the rapport we experience in our relationships with other people. It is frequently suggested that the inability to form harmonious relationships is a major cause of unhappiness, stress and anxiety. To us humans, being the social animals we are, this should come as no surprise. Even in this individualistic age, our health, material success and emotional wellbeing depend to a large extent on our ability to forge constructive relationships. This is one of the reasons why autism, which inhibits a person's inbuilt social communication abilities, is such a debilitating condition.

BASIC METHODS OF RAPPORT BUILDING: MATCHING AND MIRRORING

Fortunately, it is a relatively easy matter to improve on your ability to build rapport with other people. Rapport building techniques can be mastered fairly quickly and will have far reaching effects in your life; whether at work, at home or with friends. There are many very simple NLP techniques aimed at improving rapport. Most of these are conscious adaptations of the unconscious processes we go through when interacting with someone. These basic methods include:

- Mimicking a person's breathing pattern.
- Subtly mirroring a person's body language. (I must emphasize that subtlety is the crucial ingredient here. Obvious mirroring is immediately apparent and will often have the opposite effect to that which was intended. This is a mistake all too often made by inexperienced sales people.)

- Listen to a person's speech and use similar words to them in your responses.

The key to these basic NLP techniques is paying full attention to the person you are interacting with. People commonly do not pay attention when talking to others – they are all the while day dreaming or merely thinking of what they want to say next. Making this common mistake means that you are likely to miss out on body language and spoken signals from the other person, making effective rapport more difficult.

BEYOND THE BASICS: TUNING INTO WHETHER SOMEONE IS VISUAL, AUDITORY OR KINAESTHETIC

Timelines
There are real neurological structures that support our experience of time, past, present and future. In NLP, understanding timelines is critical to our understanding of subjective experience.

Eliciting Timelines
Everyone has an intuitive notion of time, distant past relative to recent past, the present, the near future or distant future are all arranged in some manner for each of us.

In Time **vs. Through Time**

In Time:
- Your time line goes through your body
- You are associated in the now
- You are not aware of time passing
- You tend to have associated memories
- You tend not to plan you avoid deadlines or are not good at keeping them

Through Time:
- Your time line passes outside your body
- You are dissociated from the now
- You are aware of time passing
- You tend to have dissociated memories
- You tend to plan ahead

You are aware of deadlines and are good at keeping them.

Walking and Talking the Timeline

Time is such an integral part of our experience, yet many of us feel ruled by it. Once we learn that we can traverse time in either direction, time can become a powerful *resource*.

We can travel back to the past to revisit or learn from an experience, and we can travel into the future to test outcomes before they happen.

The Language of Time is the Key to *Timeline Travel*

In language we use past, present and future tenses to communicate with ourselves where along a timeline events have occurred, are occurring, or will occur.

Walking the Timeline

It is one thing to use language to help us travel into the past, but we can amp up the experience by imagining a timeline onto which we place past or future events, and then walk into those events to experience them in a much richer way.

Sensory Experience

Experience happens via the senses. The five senses comprise the interface between our central nervous system and the external world. The NLP terms for the 5 senses are:
- **V**isual (sight)

- **A**uditory (hearing)
- **K**inesthetic (touch, pressure, heat, balance, feelings)
- **O**lfactory (smell)
- **G**ustatory (taste)

There is also a sixth sense in NLP, which is:
- **A**uditory **D**igital (self-talk)

Our senses produce neurological events, some of which are encoded as memories (especially when mixed with strong emotions), and others discarded as incidental information not worthy of memory.

Attention

Attention is the willful direction of awareness in a particular direction. Attention is something we "give" to a subject, or "pay" in order to gain some benefit. Attention is the currency of every transaction in a quantum economy. Where attention goes, energy flows.

External Attention

NLP was born by paying attention to external cues emitted from successful people that most people were simply blind to. The blindness stemmed from lack of distinctions between the thought and *behavior* patterns of successful people vs unsuccessful people.

Robert Kiyosaki has said that one of the first keys to wealth is first getting a vocabulary of wealthy people. Without the vocabulary, the mind lacks the ability to absorb, integrate and transmit information that must be used in the accumulation of wealth.

Internal Attention

The ability to pay attention to the language of the

body is critical to the health and longevity of the body. Signals given to the mind through the body and the emotions are increasingly ignored, or blunted in our society.

To open the communication channels between the body and emotions and the mind, try taking a personal inventory. With eyes closed, and in a relaxed and safe position:

- You can slowly perform an internal scan of your inner body through the beam of your awareness
- You can passively and acceptingly notice the *internal dialog* in your head
- You can notice your sense of balance and position in space
- You can notice the strength and locality of any emotions
- You can notice the noticing of these things, and notice how it is that you notice them
- If you notice any resistance to taking the time to notice these things, you can just notice this too
- You can notice yourself letting go of this internal awareness and notice the transition from internal back to external awareness.

Representational Systems

As said earlier, the senses are the interface between the outside world and the our central nervous system. As a learning organism, the external world is "re-presented" internally. Thus we form an internal sensory "map" of the external world, by which we navigate.

Our *representational system* is a living, growing and evolving whole, and to better understand the whole system, NLP divides it into its sensory components:
- The *Visual* System
- The *Auditory* System
- The *Kinesthetic* System
- The *Olfactory* System
- The *Gustatory* System
- Our *internal Dialog*

Accessing Cues

The senses bring representations of the outside world to our central nervous system, but there are also aspects of our inner experience that are broadcast to the external world. The way we move our eyes, articulate our voice, breathe, blink, blush or flush, hold our posture and gesture gives us away.

There is a universal unspoken language that help others understand what is going on inside our experience. Cartoonists capture these expressions superbly well. Some animals also read these cues very well. A dog quickly learns and thoroughly understands its dominant or submissive place within the human pack.

All but severely autistic people possess functioning mirror neurons, positioned between our motor neurons and emotional neurons, which are specialized to help us recognize these unspoken cues naturally. NLP helps us make distinctions and refine our ability to use our natural abilities better.

Unconscious Mind

The *Unconscious* Mind Holds the Keys

If you are reading this now, you have stumbled upon one of the most powerful truths of NLP, which is that *your unconscious* mind holds the keys to permanent and lasting change. You cannot produce lasting change just by thinking about it consciously. New behaviors can only be integrated and habituated when they are mixed with unconsciously held meaning and emotions, and when there are no other unconscious programs that would override or preempt running the new behavior.

What Goes On Down There?

For every calculation you perform in your conscious mind, there are millions of calculations happening below your level of present awareness. Just to stay alive, *your unconscious* mind scans the *environment* for changes from moment to moment, using all of the 5 senses. *Your unconscious* thresholds are constantly set and reset, based on prior experience, *leading* up to and including the previous moment, and anything under threshold is left out unaware to you, while anything over threshold calls for your attention.

What Else is Down There?

Your unconscious mind also holds all of your beliefs, your memories, your coding of events in and through time, your values, your emotions, and through these structures your present moment sensory inputs are processed.

Though you cannot see *your unconscious* mental constructs directly, contrastive analysis provides the evidence that they exist. They leave a mark. For example, why is it that some people can say something and be totally believable, and others can say exactly the same thing, and be utterly distrusted? Well, the output suggests that something other than the words being said activated an unconscious filter, leading to a different response. It could have been the way the words were spoken, or something else in the environment going on when the words were spoken.

How to Work with the Unconscious Mind

Using NLP language patterns, we can probe *your unconscious* mind indirectly, via the language processing centers, and thus reveal the underlying mental constructs. We use precise language patterns to drill down to specific details held in *your unconscious*, or vague language to conjure up symbolic meanings and feelings harbored in *your unconscious* mind.

In the latter case, NLP uses *trance induction*, or *hypnosis* to confuse, occupy, relax, or otherwise bypass the conscious mind, in order to have a shorter and more direct path to *your unconscious*.

Learning

From birth, we humans are fantastic learners, learning different life lessons at different life stages. Yet as adults, there are some lessons that we never seem to learn, as evidenced by repeated mistakes, and some habits we break only hardly. Maybe you can think of one or two in your life. I certainly can think of some in my own life!

This section explores some ways to look at learning that can help us engage our natural learning abilities in pursuit of the values and goals that matter most.

Levels of Learning

Levels of learning is a simple model for helping us understand where we are in our progression of learning a new skill or body of knowledge. We all go through these stages on our way to mastery or we may stop at some point short of mastery.

When we know where we are along this progression gives us hope because we see light at the end of the tunnel, and knowing that others also go through the same stages when learning a skill we can avoid becoming discouraged along the way.

In the beginning, we don't know what we don't know, and then at the end are new skill or body of knowledge becomes putty in our hands.

Learning can traditionally be divided into 5 stages:
- *Unconscious* Incompetence
- Conscious Incompetence
- Conscious Competence
- Unconscious Competence
- Mastery

Unconscious Incompetence

This is a stage of learning where we don't know what we don't know. In this stage we are either not interested in learning because the subject is not part of our awareness, or we know so little about the subject that we overestimate our abilities or underappreciate all there is to know about the subject.

Conscious Incompetence

This stage of learning happens early on in a new endeavor and is characterized by an understanding that we have a long way to go. This stage can be daunting, and a decision must be made whether to cut bait or fish.

Conscious Competence
We go through this stage when we realize that through practice, effort and concentration we are getting results. We know what we know, and we can manipulate the *outcome* through applying what we have learned.

Unconscious Competence
This is a stage is really post-learning. We perform an act or a skill without mental effort, as though automatic. Once we learn how to ride a bike, we never have to learn again, because that skill has become unconscious, directed by our will, but we do not have to think of the mechanics involved.

Mastery
Mastery is when a skill is learned so well that we are about to produce a *state* of flow surrounding the performance. Time slows down, and other elements of creativity, and feedback from the *environment* are woven into the performance of the act.

Perceptual Positions
An important aspect of learning is the developed ability to see things from multiple points of view. To only see things from one's own point of view makes one narrow-minded indeed.

Seeing things from multiple angles is crucially important for NLP practitioners, but also vital for all kinds of personal relationships as well. NLP formally names these positions:

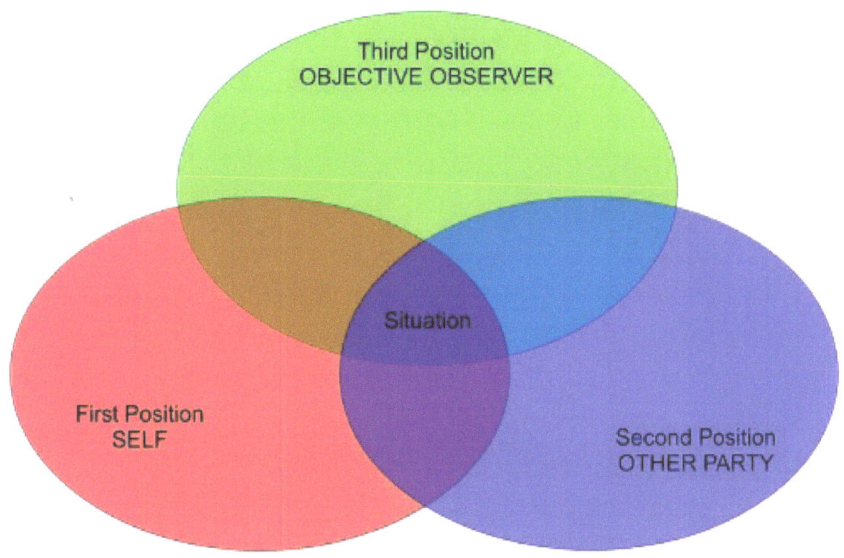

First Position
First position is the default position for everybody. It is me and my story, my wants, my needs, my position and my point of view. There is nothing wrong with first position, however being limited to first position is a guaranteed way to cut oneself off socially.

Second Position
Second position is the you in I and you. When relating to another person, it is essential to elevate that person from an object or "it" to a you, or even a thou. This is achieved when we focus our attention on the other person to the degree that we are able to see as they see, hear as they hear, and feel as they feel. Taking the second perceptual position is effective any time, but most powerfully effective when taken in real time. That is in the presence of the other person.

In relationships that really matter, we need to be sure that we "walk a mile in their shoes". NLP provides wonderful exercises, where for an hour or a day, we actually walk and talk and think like the other person, in order to adopt their persona on a temporary basis. Under *hypnosis*, the NLP practitioner may also encourage the client in a relationship to circle around, and then float down into the body of their partner, in order to experience their world through their senses. From time to time Gandhi also assumed the perspectives of the Indian, the Muslim, and the British, in deep meditation, whose conflicting vistas needed reconciliation.

Contrast the presidencies of Abraham Lincoln, who filled his cabinet with many dissenters from his own point of view, with that of George W. Bush, where dissenting opinions were few and far between. One may not be in agreement with other points of view, but when the stakes are high, we must take pains to take those other points of view under advisement.

Third Position

Third position is when we are able to imagine ourselves relating to another party, but observing that relating as an independent and unbiased bystander. The point of this exercise is to be able watch the dynamics going on between oneself, the other person, and not have any stake in the *outcome*, except to learn from the observation. Businesses often invite meeting moderators to observe the meeting, set ground rules, and provide feedback on the quality of the interactions in the meeting, rather than participating in the discussion itself. Family and relationship counselors also play the role of third position observer, when conflicting views are being expressed.

It's difficult, though very profitable, to take the third

position in one's own relationship, but in doing so, one must make sure to completely abandon any biases towards one party or the other. As you imagine yourself as the unbiased observer, check to be sure that your position is spatially at a midpoint between both parties, and that both parties seem equal in size, position, volume, influence, etc.

Our Collective Social Mind
In NLP, it is useful not only to study our individual minds, but also how our minds function and evolve as a collective. We are open systems, and so it is impossible not to be influenced by our *environment*, and by interacting with other minds.
Neurological Levels

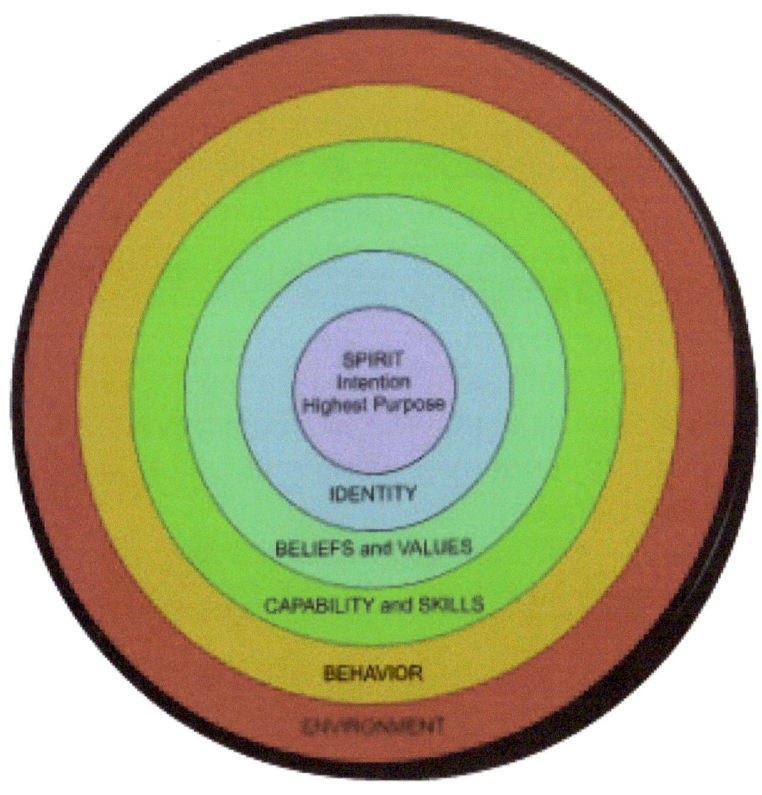

Remember at all times that *the map is not the territory*. Still, there are many models in NLP that can help us share our maps of the world. We owe a debt to Robert Dilts for helping to develop one such model for understanding behaviors, motivations, and relationships called *Neurological Levels*. The levels are:
- *Environment*
- Behavior
- *Capability*
- Beliefs and Values
- *Identity*
- Spirituality

As important as the levels are for understanding ourselves and our drivers, it is equally beneficial to study the boundaries and interactions between the levels.

Environment

The environment is everything surrounding us, beginning with the air and objects in direct contact with us, and extends to the farthest reaches of the universe. It is where we work, sleep, eat, play, and interact with others. We impact the environment at all times, and the environment also shapes us. There are no neutralities in this interaction. Every word we hear, every sight we see is perceived by some level, though not everything makes it into our *conscious* awareness.

On the level of environment, we can have some degree of superficial *rapport* through familiar surroundings.

Linguistically, we might understand the impact of the environment on a person by listening to the predicates such as "I can't do that *here*".

Behavior

At the boundary of behavior and environment is the physiological impact of one on the other. If our environment is stressful, our physiology responds with fight or flight mechanisms. If we demonstrate pleasing behavior, the environment and others welcome our presence.

Behavior is the only part of another person that we can directly observe. It is the *surface structure* under which there is hidden or deeper structures that we use *modeling* to reveal.

Linguistically, we describe behavior by using predicates such as "I *sometimes do* that", or "she *moved* in here chair".

A leader who focuses on changing behavior is a *coach*.

Capability

Capability can be indirectly observed through behavior, but when someone is able to repeatably demonstrate control over their behavior and achieve a consistent *outcome*, we say they have capability or skill.

Linguistically, a person may show they operate from the level of capability by using predicates such as "I *can't* do that", or "That's *easy*".

A leader who focuses on increasing capability is a *teacher*.

Beliefs

Beliefs are filters we substitute for lack of direct knowledge of something. Beliefs may be deep-rooted and immovable (like the sun will rise tomorrow), or shallow and replaceable in the face of new evidence (like the *mismatching* socks that seemed to be the same color in the dim morning light are obviously not the same color in the light of the office).

Beliefs shape which capabilities we develop, by placing a measure of importance on those skills we perceive as necessary to survive or get ahead in life.

Linguistically, a persons may reveal his or her motivations or decisions by using predicates such as "I *shouldn't* do that", or "*if* this *then* that.

A leader who changes hearts is a *mentor*.

Identity

Identity is "me and my story". Identity is an amalgamation of defining experiences and a measure self-adulation (or at times self-flagellation).

Identity and beliefs interact constantly, and one shapes the other. Sometimes one is Yin and the other Yang, and sometimes vice versa.

Linguistically, a person who operates from the level of identity would stress predicates such as "*I* can't do that", or "that's just who *I am*". You might also hear it as "*I am the customer*", which is situational, but implies a lot about which roles everyone is expected to play in that situation.

A leader who supports the soul is a *sponsor*.

Spirit

There is a saying in Quantum Linguistics that says "no matter what you think you are, you're always more than that". This is predicated on the notion that the boundary between what is "you", and what is "not you" is an artificial construct defined only by the notion held in mind at any time. The boundary is constantly shifting as our thoughts about ourselves shift. When we stop thinking in terms of boundaries, then there are no boundaries.

This is where intention and purpose enter in.

Intention and purpose permeate all the roles we play because intention has no boundaries, though the denser forms of identity, beliefs, capabilities and behaviors often mask the presence or appearance of intention.

A leader in the realm of spirit is an *awakener*.

Spiral Dynamics
Spiral Dynamics was a term that later summarized the work of Clare Graves, as he unfolded the evolution of the human mind across many hundreds of past generations to the present.

Hero's Journey
Joseph Campbell has helped the world recontextualize that way we see ourselves and others, by borrowing from myths and legends of cultures the world over. His message, we are more alike than unlike each other.

The Hero's Journey is a universal story wherein each of us leaves or is pushed out of the naivete of our familiar surroundings, feelings, circumstances or beliefs, whereupon we have to rapidly learn to draw upon the support of strange helpers and reach deep within ourselves to cope with the new situation, then after some time we return to be able to tell the tale.

Network Science
As above, so below.

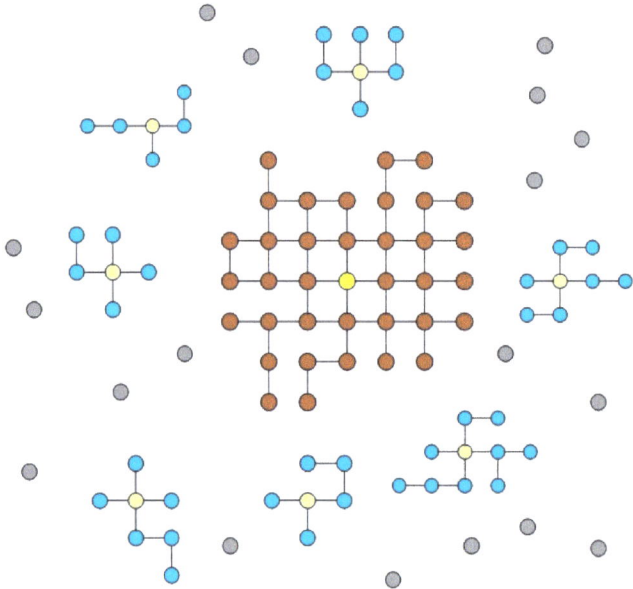

As humans, we are part of an endless, complex series of networks.
Think of dark matter and gravity on the universal scale.
Think of the food chain, the internet, social and terrorist networks and bibliographies on the human scale. Think of neurons in our nervous systems, phase shifts in chemistry, the interactions of genes in cancer formation or prevention, and so on at the molecular scale. Think of entanglement and string theory at the quantum level, and you will begin to appreciate how the complex interaction or relationships between bodies or nodes affects everything in our lives, much more than the bodies themselves.
It's the glue that matters!
For centuries, science has gone down the path of

reductionism to try to discover the ultimate truth, which consisted of breaking big things into smaller and smaller things to try to find the indivisible units of which everything else was made. At one time, atoms were believed to be the smallest particles, then science discovered electrons, protons, neutrons, and then smaller and smaller particles and wave functions, and the quest goes on. However, when you just examine the parts, there are so many answers missing. Answers that lie in the relationships between the parts. This is what network science is all about.

What are the organizing principles behind networks? What are the vulnerabilities of different network structures? What are the potential benefits to emerge from understanding networks better?

Going beyond the fundamentals, it is also possible, with a bit of practice, to assess the person's primary means of sensory perception. For instance, is the person mainly relying on their visual, auditory or kinesthetic senses? Once you have figured it out, you can rapidly enhance your rapport with the person by using the same means of perception yourself.

This is easier than it sounds and starts with paying attention to the sort of words your conversation partner is using.

VISUAL PERCEPTION

You can gauge whether your partner is primarily using visual perception if they habitually employ phrases and words related to vision, light, color and size. For instance:

"I see what you mean"
"The way I see it…"
"The answer was blindingly obvious"
"It was clear what she meant."
"The dress was dazzling"
"He was a colorful character."
"My vision is clear"
"Your future is bright"
Big
Dark
Orange
Square
Light

AUDITORY PERCEPTION

In a similar vein, if a person is primarily relying on their sense of hearing, it will be reflected in words and phrases associated with sound, hearing and noise. Listen out for examples such as these:

"I hear what you are saying"
"Her voice was loud"
"He scratched the surface"
"I'm listening to you"
"They were deaf to her advice."
"That doesn't sound good."
"Actions speak louder than words."
sound
beeping
ticking
tapping
noise

KINAESTHETIC PERCEPTION

If the person you are talking too uses abundant words or phrases relating to the sense of touch, you can be confident that they are relying on kinesthetic perception. Take these words and phrases as examples:

"I feel that it's the right thing to do"
"I have a bad feeling about this"
"She had a pleasant vibe"
"It is a really sticky situation."

warm
cool
sandy
wet
touch

Although there is no absolute science of building rapport and approaches will vary from individual to individual, the methods outlined here are foundational techniques that can be applied to almost any scenario. With practice, they will encourage an attitude of attention to the person you are talking to which in itself encourage the building of rapport.

Furthermore, by sympathetically mirroring the person's words, movements and perceptual bias you make it easier to express a genuine and instinctive empathy with the people you meet; thus laying the foundation for strong, enriching relationships.

The first step towards getting more friends is building a good rapport in the beginning of the relationship.

Whether you're trying to hit it off with your new coworkers, endear yourself on a first date, or get in a professor's good graces, you are looking to build rapport. Rapport is that feeling that you and another person are somewhat in sync because the two of you have something in common and are, in some way, alike. This isn't a quick process for most people, but it truly can be. The following tips can help you take connect with important people quickly and easily in almost every situation.

DO YOUR HOMEWORK
If you can, find out what you might have in common with the other party before you meet. Once you are armed with this information, you should let the other person know as soon as possible about any shared interests you might have as discreetly as possible. He or she shouldn't know that you have been doing any research!
If you are on a job interview, for example, scour the company's website and other internet resources to get as much information as you can about the interviewer. If you both attended the same university, served in the military or lived in the same town, subtly mention that as soon as possible, maybe even weave that into the answer of one of the questions he or she may ask. You might not be able to get any information on the interviewer, so be very knowledgeable about the company and don't be afraid to flaunt it; he or she works for the firm and you want a job there, the two of you have so much in common already!

ASK QUESTIONS FIRST
Before you start talking about yourself, ask questions about the other person in an attempt to see what you could have in common. When you are asked direct questions, answer, but be sure to

follow up immediately with a related question for the individual you're speaking with.

Don't just ask any questions, but use these queries to direct the conversation. If you just went on vacation, ask them about their last vacation. After they tell you about a trip to London, you could say something like, "I love London, but I went to Paris last month, and it was amazing. I just love to travel, don't you?"

It might not always be appropriate to talk about vacations, so stay on point. Also, remember to actually *listen* to what the other person is saying. If the other party states that they hate to travel, the above example wouldn't be an appropriate response, but you could say something that, while not a lie, is more in line with their sentiment like, "I was in Paris last month, and my flight home was delayed a whole day! What a pain!"

Linguistics

Language Creates our World in NLP

Language or Linguistics is the "L" in NLP. Language defines our subjective world, and is the key that opens all the doors in NLP.

Heidegger said "Language is the House of Being". Certainly, language is a HUGE part of what it means to be human. It is what allows us to encode experience in a way that it can be played back to ourselves as *internal dialog*, and also shared with others, in both speaking and writing.

Robert Kiyosaki says the way to attract wealth is to start by increasing one's vocabulary for wealth. Without the words to describe wealth, it is impossible to experience it.

Additionally, there are examples of cultures whose language determines the richness of experiences. The Eskimo language has 14 words for snow, which each encode a rich set of attributes and behaviors and conditions into each word. English, in contrast has one word for it.

In Sanskrit, there are more than 10 words for love. In English we use the word love very loosely, applying it to people, possessions and experiences alike. In Spanish, the word for love is reserved for the most intimate relationships.

Language As a *Representational System*

In NLP, language is a representational system, and like the other representational systems in our internal maps, it is not the territory. Language can describe a person, place, thing, event, process, feeling, sight or sound, but it is none of those things. Language is like the finger pointing at the moon, but it is not the moon.

Language exists because we are equipped both to encode our experiences in language (a sequence of sounds), and decode those sounds as a new experience. The encoding of speech is controlled by a small area in the left frontal lobe (for most right-handed people) called Broca's Area, and the decoding of speech is controlled by a small area in the left temporal lobe (again, for most right-handed people) called Wernicke's Area. We know this due to observations of brain activity, and the loss of these abilities when damage to these areas occurs. So wired are we to learn language, that we pick it up effortlessly as young children. So sensitive are we to language that we can separate out sounds from a vast variety of other sounds in our *environment*. So integrated are the speech centers in our neurology, that that every word we hear sets in motion a chain reaction in other areas of our brain involving emotions, pictures, memories, etc. Especially powerful words are those phased as questions. When we hear a question, we can't *not* try to answer it internally.

Why Language in NLP?

Because language is a shared phenomenon, we use language to "communicate" between people. Language helps us convey the rich but invisible and inaudible world of our subjective experiences to others, at risk that they may either understand our subjective world... or not... and so language is a risky proposition. When we communicate, we commune with others. When we miscommunicate or fail to communicate, we risk some degree of ostracism.

NLP practitioners use language to explore subjective experience, such as when using meta-model language patterns, whose focus is on precision of understanding. NLP also uses language to change subjective experience, such as when using persuasive, hypnotic or Milton-model language patterns. Note that whether chunking down, up or sideways in NLP work, it is the subjective experience of the person that we are communicating with. We cannot communicate *with* empical facts, but *we* can communicate with people *about* empirical facts, and thereby not change the facts themselves, but the aboutness of those facts.

NLP practitioners use language to change people by *intentionally* changing their subjective experiences in ways that establish and support positive outcomes. Language is the key toolset for the NLP practitioner to do this. With language, skilled NLP the practitioner can lead a journey into the past, change the qualities of that subjective past, *install* resourceful thinking into that past in a way that it ie re-experienced in a new way, resulting in a re-imprinted or changed subjective person. With language, the skilled NLP practitioner can create a more focused or diffused outlook on present circumstances in order to help the subjective experience sort for opportunities, forgiveness, elimination of pain, beauty or any other quality of present moment experience that would normally escape the notice of someone. With language, a skilled NLP practitioner can lead a journey into the future, where clear and ecological outcomes are established and fixed to a certain future date and circumstance, such that the steps towards that outcome are inspired by its inevitable attainment.

NLP Training: Meta Model Language Patterns

The Yang of Language Patterns

The Meta-Model is also known as the language of precision, or precision language, which addresses the common tendency of people to sometimes overgeneralize, distort or delete information as we speak and write.

First inspired in the NLP founders by modeling Virginia Satir in her therapeutic work, the *Meta Model* is a deductive language model which emphasizes the general to the specific. The meta model is used as a tool to reveal additional meaning that is hidden under the surface of what is being said.

The Meta Model is characterized by good questioning that reveals meaning behind what is initially being said. Questions like:

- What, specifically?
- Who, specifically?
- When, specifically?
- How, specifically?

Sometimes our problems are allowed to persist and propagate on their own momentum because they thrive in a kind of *trance state*. Meta Model language patterns are used to interrupt those kinds of thoughts and shed more light on the finer distinctions that may have been ignored while in trance. For example:

Problem: My partner does not love me because she never pays attention to me. **Meta Model:** Never EVER pays attention? How specifically does that mean she does not love you?

Problem: I'll never get a promotion. **Meta Model:**

How specifically do you know you will never get a promotion? How does that mean you will never get a promotion?

You get the point. These lines of questioning are very useful when working with others in a stuck state, and particularly useful in examining our own stuck states, which need to be challenged in order to progress to more resourceful states.

NLP Training: Milton Model Language Patterns

The Yin of Language Patterns
The Milton-Model was named for Milton Erickson by the NLP founders, who were introduced to Milton Erickson by Gregory Bateson. The *Milton Model* is a broad variety of
persuasive and hypnotic language patterns that move one from the specific toward the general in search of solutions that have been overlooked under one's present model or map of the world. Milton Erickson was a world-famous hypnotherapist, whose use of *metaphor*, oblique references, vague and permissive language was able to effectively bypass the critical faculties of his

clients, and work directly on the subconscious mind. By using vague and permissive language in his suggestions, the client would feel as though they themselves could come up with solutions to their presenting problems, which was indeed the case.

Volumes have been written on the topic of Milton Erickson's language, and it is very profitable to learn. We are indebted to Tad James for the following summary of Milton patterns:

1. *Mind Read*: Asserting that one knows the thoughts or feelings of another without specifying the process by which you came to know their thoughts.
Example: "I know that you want to know..." - *Meta Model* Antidote: "How do you know that?"

2. Lost Performative: *Value* judgments (which may include an unspecified comparison) where the performer of the value judgment is left out.
Example: *"And it's a good thing to wonder..."* - Meta Model Antidote: *"Who says it's a good thing?"*

3. Cause and Effect: Where it is implied that one thing causes another.
Examples: If... then... As you... then you... *"Because..."* - Meta Model Antidote: *"Are you sure about the cause of that?"*

4. *Complex Equivalence*: Where two things are equated – as in their meanings being equivalent.
Example: *"That means..."* - Meta Model Antidote: *"How specifically does this mean that...?"*

5. Presupposition: The linguistic equivalent of assumptions.
Example: *"You are learning many things..."* - Meta Model Antidote: *"How did you know that?"*

6. Universal Quantifier: A set of words which has:
Examples: *"And everything, always..."* - Meta Model Antidote: *"Really? Everything? Everyone?, Always?"*

7. *Modal Operator*: Words, which implies possibility or necessity, which often form our rules in life.
Example: *"That you can, should, must learn..."* - Meta Model Antidote: *"Why do you need to do that now?"*

8. *Nominalization*: Process words (including verbs), which have been frozen *in time* by making them into nouns.
Example: *"...new insights, and new understandings."* - Meta Model Antidote: *"How is it specifically that you come to see or understand?"*

9. Unspecified Verb: Where an adjective or adverb modifier does not specify the verb.
Example: *"And you can, happily."* - Meta Model Antidote: *"And I can **what**, happily?"*

10. Tag Question: A question added after a statement, designed to displace resistance with tacit agreement.
Example: *"Is is not?"* - Meta Model Antidote: *"No, it is not."*

11. Lack of Referential Index: A phrase, which

does not pick out a specific portion of the listener's experience.
Example: *"One can, you know..."* - Meta Model Antidote: *"One can what?"*

12. Comparative *Deletion* (Unspecified Comparison): Where the comparison is made and it is not specified as to what or whom it was made.
Example: *"And it's more or less the right thing."* - Meta Model Antidote: *"More or less than what?"*

13. *Pacing* Current Experience: Where client's verifiable, external experience is described in a way, which is undeniable.
Example: "You are sitting here, listening to me, looking at me, (etc.)..."

14. Double Bind: Where the client is given two choices (both of which are preferable or desired) separated by an "or".
Example: *"I don't know whether you'll come to realize it earlier or later..."* - Meta Model Antidote: *"Who says I'll come to know it ever?"*

15. Conversational Postulate: The communication has the form of a question – a question to which the response is either a 'yes' or a 'no'. If I want you to do something, what else must be present so that you will do it, and out of your awareness? It allows you to choose to respond or not and avoids authoritarianism.
Example: "Do you feel this is something you understand?"

16. Extended Quotes: Quotes which are extended

beyond what is normally used to displace resistance.
Example: "Last week I was with a friend, who told me about something he overheard his co-worker say..."

17. Selectional Restriction Violation: A sentence that is not well formed in that only humans and animals can have feelings.
Examples: "A chair can feel sat on, like a doormat can feel stepped on..."

18a. *Phonological Ambiguity*: Where two words with different meanings sound the same. IE: "Hear", "Here"

18b. *Syntactic Ambiguity*: Where the function (syntactic) of a word cannot be immediately determined from the immediate *context*.
Examples: "They are visiting relatives" "Selling salesmen can be tricky!" "I am really over managing managers."

18c. Scope Ambiguity: Where it cannot be determined by linguistic context how much is applied to that sentence by some other portion of the sentence.
Examples: *"Speaking to you as a child..."* "The old men & women..." "The disturbing noises & thoughts..." "The weight of your hands & feet..."

18d. Punctuation Ambiguity: Either the punctuation is eliminated as in a run on sentence or pauses occur in the wrong place.
Example: "I want you to notice your hand me the

glass."

19. Utilization: Remember to utilize all that happens or is said.
Example: Client says: "I am not sold." Response: "That's right you are not sold, yet, because you haven't *asked the one question that will have you totally and completely sold."*

Putting it all together:
"I know that you are wondering... and it's a good thing to wonder... because... that means... you are learning many things... and all the things, all the things... that you can learn... provide you with new insights, and new understandings. And you can, can you not? One can, you know. And it's more or less the right thing. You are sitting here, listening to me, looking at me, and that means that your *unconscious* mind is also here, and can hear what I say. And since that's the case, you are probably learning about this and already know more at an unconscious level than you think you do, and it's not right for me to tell him, learn this or learn that, let him learn in any way he wants, in any order. Do you feel this... is something you understand? Because, last week I was with Milton who told me about his training in 1979 in Miami when he talked to someone who said, "A chair can have feelings..."

NLP Training: Sleight of Mouth Language Patterns

The NLP term "*Sleight of Mouth*" came into being through Robert Dilts' observations of Richard Bandler, who was expert at responding to complex equivalent (X means Y) challenges in ways that quickly reframed that challenge to provide an alternate meaning, and steered the dialogue in a new direction.

Example Challenge

"You are late again, and that means you don't care!"

One could simply apologize for being late, but that would not address the meaning the other person has attached to the lateness. Sleight of Mouth patterns do this.

Sleight of Mouth Responses

- "You are only saying that because you are not considering our whole relationship."
- "Sorry, I was just thinking how much I love you... what was that?"
- "That kind of response first thing makes me want to stay at the office a little longer."
- "If I risked driving faster on the ice to get here sooner, that would be taking the short view."
- "How late is late?"
- "Does everyone have to be home at a certain time to show that they care about their relationship?"
- "You're only bringing it up because you feel unloved, is that right?"
- "Being on time is not the same as caring. Enemies can be on time and not care."
- "Have you always been on time?"
- "What is really important about being on time, and what is really important about caring?"
- "How specifically does not being on time mean that I don't care?"
- "There was once this person who had to choose between two difficult choices... help a stranger or keep a prior commitment... "

- "Being on time is not the real issue... whether I love you is the heart of the matter, right?"
- "Having a terrific relationship is what we're really shooting for here, right?"

Notice that some of the patterns are slippery, and others are outright confrontational. You must use these with care!

Programming
Programming Is the Craft of NLP

It's no coincidence that Richard Bandler was a computer programmer at the time he coined the term "Neuro Linguistic **Programming**". By that time, he understood that our *unconscious* minds ran programs developed, compiled and executed in our neurology from a accumulation of our past experiences.

In Richard Bandler's and John Grinder's pursuit of understanding excellence, they came to realize that programs or strategies of healing or excellence in people ran all by themselves in people, even though they themselves did not know how those programs worked. Just like you and I can use computer programs to achieve our goals without ever having to see or understand the code running underneath those programs.

So if John and Richard could learn the code to those programs, they would be able to adapt and *install* those programs on the neurological operating systems of other people.

NLP Programs Address Three Questions

Would you buy a piece of software that did not do what you needed it to? Of course not? You want to make sure that the program satisfies your

computing requirements, and does its job well.
In NLP neurological programs are no different. We want to make sure the programs work well in our real lives. So we start out by asking three questions:

- What do you want... exactly? What is your desired *outcome*?
- Where are you now? How exactly do you do the things that are not working now?
- What is the best, most effective, efficient, ecological and enjoyable way to get what you want, given your operating system? What other choices can we create for you now?

Based on the answers to these questions, NLP can design and build a program that can then be installed into one's neurology that allows a person to move through the world in the direction of those things that they really want to have, do, or be.

People Are Not Broken, Our Programs Are Outdated

If what we are doing is not working, NLP does not say the person is broken. NLP says instead that we need some new programs... programs that lead to better results. This is the work of NLP. We design, test, install and support new programs that work better in people, in their real lives. Sometimes our strategies need to be replaced. Other times, our strategies just need a bug fix or an upgrade. Sometimes we need to search for and destroy thought viruses that are interfering with the functioning of strategies that otherwise would work well.

And just like a programmer would approach the a computer system to decide what is needed before designing a new software program, a Neuro

Linguistic Programmer would also approach the programs running in the neurology... or the conscious and unconscious mind.
This section deals with the major components of our neurological programs. Outcomes, Strategies and States.

NLP Outcomes
NLP Sensory-Based Outcomes
In NLP, an outcome is more than a goal. An outcome includes sensory-based evidence, such that you *know* when you have reached an outcome because the outcome is recognizable by your senses. In other words, based on what you can see, hear, feel, smell or taste, how do you know you have reached your outcome? To use a barbecue as an example... what do perfectly cooked chops look, sound and smell like before you remove them from the grill? Without these *submodalities* as a guide we run the risk of over or under-cooking the chops.

Just Ask
It all starts with getting clear or sure about what do you want to learn or have, or where you want to go. Invest the time to see the sights, hear the sounds, and feel the feelings not of having completed the last step on the way to the outcome. For example, if your outcome is to enjoy Niagra Falls (known by some to be the *second* biggest disappointment of the honeymoon), then visualize yourself driving through the gates of the parking lot on either the American or the Canadian side and paying the parking fee in the local currency.

Outcome thinking vs. Problem Thinking

This is a key difference between successful people versus people in stuck states. A problem-orientation or outlook results in behaviors of blame or other kinds of inaction. Outcome thinking charts a course from the problem state to the outcome state, and then uses sensory feedback to decide when steps toward the outcome are actually completed successfully. The outcome is assured before it even happens.

Outcome-oriented thinkers look at a problem as something to be understood and clarified, because they know that a problem well-stated is a problem half solved. Then the rest of the steps toward the desired outcome become action oriented.

With this background, let's dive a little deeper into outcomes.

Life Mission

A life mission is the kind of *outcome* that shapes one's entire life. A life mission has these characteristics:
- Long Term
- Clear and Compelling
- Connect with Core Values and *Identity*
- Emotionally Compelling
- Seem Impossible at First
- Do not Require Sacrifice of Present Moment for Future Outcome

It is not surprising to learn that many people go through life, never having discovered the specific purpose they were born to do.

For those people, we highly recommend the use of

the Path Primer from Brain Technologies, as a starting point for discovering one's purpose. Once one's purpose becomes clear, it is quite amazing how all other aspects of one's life align themselves to support that purpose. Then NLP really becomes a powerful tool for helping to energize and move a person forward in achieving that purpose.

SMART Goals

Goals are measurable outcomes that one sets, achieves, and then crosses off a list, or conversely that one forgets about, drops or leaves for a different or modified goal.

SMART Goals share the following characteristics:
- **S**pecific/**S**imply-written/**S**ensory-based
- **M**easurable/**M**eaningful to Me
- **A**s If Now/**A**ttainable/**A**llowed
- **R**ealistic/**R**esponsible
- **T**ime-bound/**T**oward What I Want

How to Write Goals

Written as: "It is now _____, I am / I have _____."

- It is now August 08, 2008, I am standing on the scale, I weigh 125 lbs.
- It is now January 1, 2014, I am writing the check on my last house payment.
- It is now January 1, 2014, I am resigning from my IT consulting job for a career in music.

Future *Pacing*

When you set a goal, it is important to envision oneself having achieved the goal, and try on the outcome for size. This process allows for tweaking the goal should any incongruences be discovered, and can in some cases help one see that the goal itself may be incongruent with other larger goals, so that the goal can be scrapped before investing too much time or effort in it. If the goal checks out with one's own parts and with the other stake holders, then proceed to implement it.

Releasing Resistance

One final step often overlooked is to identify barriers, blockages, resistance or "why not's" that may arise and eventually sabotage a great goal. A fantastic exercise, then, is to *future pace* the goal, bring up any felt resistance, big or small, and release that resistance to discharge any negative emotions associated with achieving the goal. Rather than denying that barriers do exist, one can use this exercise to plan for them in advance, and replace any foreseen shame, apathy, grief, fear, anger, or pride with more positive emotions of courage, acceptance or peace.

Structuring Outcomes

Express in positive terms:
- What do you want?

Gather evidence of direction or arrival?
- How will you know if you are succeeding or have succeeded?

Know the Specifics:
- Where, when and with whom?

Know your Resources:
- Ideas
- Money
- Information, Familiarity
- Role Models
- Talents, Personal Attributes

Control:
- How much can you do yourself?
- How much will you need others?

Ecology:
- What is the cost?
- What are the wider consequences?

Identity:
- Is this consistent with who I am (we are)?

Congruency:
- Are there any parts not in agreement?

Action Plan:
- What are the next steps?

Beliefs and Outcomes

Beliefs are the rules we act on. Beliefs are a powerful system inside our neurology, stand in for knowledge, and help us to operate in an uncertain world where we do not have all the information. Without beliefs we would be paralyzed, literally. Relative to outcomes, beliefs act as sails, anchors and rudders. Beliefs can be the engine that powers us forward, the brakes that slow us down or stop us, or the steering wheel that help to change course.

In a quantum sense, our beliefs determine the boundaries of the possibilities that will express themselves in our experience. Beliefs can open tremendous opportunities, or narrow our ability to perceive opportunities in plain sight.

The better acquainted we become with our own beliefs as forces in our lives, the better equipped we will be to abandon disempowering beliefs, and *install* empowering ones.

In NLP we recogniza that to support the achievement of a desired outcome, beliefs about the outcome should pass the PAW criterion:
- I believe it is **P**ossible for me to achieve the outcome.

- I believe I am **A**ble to achieve the outcome.
- I believe I am **W**orthy to achieve the outcome. I deserve it.

When these criterion are met, one is literally able to walk into the outcome. If any of these criterion are absent in a belief about the outcome, at some level we tend to find ourselves losing momentum or sabotaging efforts to achieve the outcome.

The good news about beliefs from NLP is that beliefs that do not serve one in moving towards and achieving a worthy outcome can be changed.

NLP Strategies
In NLP, Strategies Link the Mind with the Body

In NLP, a mind and body that is not running strategies, or mental patterns, is asleep or dead... in which case we really don't need NLP. But for those of us that are alive and awake, it's profitable to understand how strategies in the mind and body work in real time and in the real world.

In NLP, strategies are what we do neurologically to get what we want. So strategies have both mental and physiological components based in our neurology. Strategies are a sequence of representational building blocks in our mind that lead to an *outcome*. These strategies may be *conscious* or *unconscious*.

Here is an example: If I *see* a piece of chocolate cake, I might *imagine* how much I would like it and begin to *salivate*, and so I *walk* over and *take a bite*. Seeing and imagining, salivating, walking and eating are all connected in a *strategy* that has a beginning, a certain sequence and and end. Here is a more complex version of a strategy that includes more choice: I *see* a piece of chocolate cake, and I might *imagine* how much I would like it and begin to *salivate*, but then I *check* how full my stomach *feels*, and *remember* that I have a date at the gym soon, and so I *decide* to hydrate with a glass of cool water instead.

Components of Strategies

In NLP, we study the structure, sequence and components of neurological strategies including:
- **External Stimuli**, or triggers and anchors in the *environment*
- **Internal States**, or alertness and emotions
- **Representational Systems**, including sensory modes and their *submodalities*
- **External Behaviors**, including all physiological responses

Categories of Strategies

There are all kinds of strategies that we have as human beings, including:
- **Decision Strategies**, or how we decide for or against something
- **Motivation Strategies**, or how we decide to move toward or away from something
- **Learning Strategies**, or how we accumulate and organize information
- **Reality Strategies**, or how we know what is real and what is not
- **Memory Strategies**, or how we *chunk* and recall information we have leaned

Reasons for Understanding Strategies

If we know the components, and categories of strategies, we can effectively program changes to them in order to get a better outcome. Precisely at the point in a strategy that is not working, we can snip out a part of a strategy, insert another option, bring in new information, or rearrange the sequence of steps, in order allow a person to unconsciously and naturally achieve a better result. If NLP Practitioners think like programmers, and think of strategies as neurological code, then they will also understand how and where to make changes to that code. That is what this section deals with.

This section addresses how we use the components of strategies within each category of strategy in order to make changes where necessary to get what we want. We are changing the way the mind works, including its links to the body, and hence produce a different outcome in the real world.

MATCHING AND MIRRORING

The foundation of rapport is not simply having something in common, but being like the other person. When folks are really hitting it off they start to act and talk like each other! You can try to mirror someone's speech and actions to speed up the process of building rapport.

The key to this is subtlety. If you make this obvious, the other person could realize you are copying them and think that you are mocking them. When trying to mirror actions, be discreet. Mirror small gestures or movements that are probably subconscious for the other person. Touch your cheek when they do. If they cross their legs, do the same. When they take a drink of water, you take a drink from your glass. You don't have to do *everything* they do, as you might look a bit crazy, but just a few simple actions should be more than enough.

If you try to copy someone's speech, don't attempt

to copy accents. Instead, focus first on their speed. If he or she speaks slowly or quickly, do the same. Some people might use a certain vocabulary, favoring specific words that you can start to pepper your speech with. You can also pick up on cadence; for example, if someone's speech is singsong, you could start speaking in the same way. Again, don't attempt to copy accents, and please also avoid speech impediments and mispronunciations, as you run a <u>very</u> high risk of offending.

Building rapport is an important step in any relationship, and it can be done quickly and easily in almost every situation. By establishing rapport quickly, you stand a better chance of landing the job, getting a second date or being remembered for the next big business deal.

2. DISSOCIATION

Much of the stress, depression and negative emotions we experience in day-to-day life are the result of trigger reactions to common experiences. For instance, you may notice your temper rising whenever you hear someone mention a particular word or phrase. Alternatively, it may be a particular habit of your partner's that sends you into a paroxysm of rage or inertia.

Dissociation essentially severs the link between the negative state of mind and the trigger event. As such it is a very effective long term treatment for deeply entrenched psychological issues such as anxiety, depression, stress and phobias. It is also a positive way of dealing with difficulties at work, home or in our relationships.

Association vs. Dissociation

Every experience is perceived to happen at some point along a continuum of *association* [1] vs. *dissociation* [2]. Association is when the experience is felt to be part of you, or that you are part of the experience. You seem to be identified with the experience or connected somehow with it. Dissociation is when you feel you are watching, listening to or observing the an event from the outside.

The properties of association vs. dissociation are such a powerful component of any experience that we can transform the experience itself. This is true of past experiences, our present moment experience, and even a future possible experience.

Association

Association is useful when you want to feel more connected or one with a present pleasant experience, a past powerful experience, or a future desirable *state* [3].

The language of association is:
- Step into _____
- Try _____ on for size
- See what you saw, hear what you heard and feel what you felt when _____
- Turn up the volume, make it bigger and brighter!

Dissociation

Dissociation is useful when you want to feel free from past pain, present stress, or when there is a future goal toward which you want to be motivated.

The language of dissociation is:
- Move away from _____
- Float above _____
- Move around to the other side of _____

- Observe yourself in that situation again doing _____

Shrink that image, dim it, make the voice further away

3. CONTENT REFRAME

Content Reframe is a group of visualization techniques that encourages you to think differently about situations in which you feel disempowered, victimized or out of control. The technique allows you to view negative situations in a new light, and thus enables you to see how positive outcomes might be derived from seemingly hopeless and frustrating situations.

This NLP technique can be of benefit to people who have experienced severe trauma in their past such as battlefield stress or childhood abuse—or who are suffering from chronic or life-threatening illness. Content Reframe is also useful for helping you deal with acute and unexpected trauma, such as losing a job or suffering bereavement.

We All Experience Self-Hypnosis Every Day

Trance is a naturally occurring state that we all do several times daily. During waking hours, there are times when we find ourselves relaxed and daydreaming, with our critical faculties and inhibitions diminished, as we go into a state of heightened learning, or suggestibility. Trance is like a daydream where we suspend our critical judge in order to allow new solutions to arise. Sometimes this trance happens all by itself, but learning to do Self-Hypnosis is a powerful creative tool that we can call on as needed.

Kids Learn Naturally in a State of Light Hypnotic Trance

Until about the age of 6, young children are in a slightly hypnotic state nearly all the time. Their brain is dominated by alpha waves, which are characteristically present during states of rapid learning. The brains of young children are very "plastic", designed to absorb information, social norms, values and language very quickly, but those same young brains lack the critical reasoning abilities that come with age and experience, and only when they are able to move out of alpha into sustained beta wave patterns. Recall tha children's brains are also quite imaginative, and the ability to distinguish reality from fiction is quite blurred. Notice also that this is the period where language is most naturally developed.

Adults Enter Trance Several Times a Day

As adults, we spend less overall time in hypnotic trances than we did as 6-year-old children, but we still spend a few minutes each hour daydreaming, integrating new learning's, reviewing future plans, reliving confrontations, or stunned by beauty, or encounters with celebrity. These are all trance states. Whenever we are required to make a foul shot, or a putt, or to spell a difficult word, we enter trance, by tuning out external stimuli. Trance is normal and healthy, and it is the only state in which we really learn anything. It is the "*downtime*" that our brains require to make sense of the new sensory inputs we are constantly bombarded with.

As adults we can use Self Hypnosis to learn rapidly, update our beliefs, and modify our map of the world. Old habits can be diminished, and beliefs and new habits established, strengthened and habituated as the critical mind is temporarily and willfully suspended.

Remember that the job of the critical mind is to evaluate the future, against the memories of the past, in the present, using a linear mental calculus. When the "*uptime*" mode of linear thinking dominates, we are in executive mode, and no learning can occur in those moments.

What Hypnosis is Not
Hypnosis is not sleep.

Sleep is dominated by Theta waves during light sleep, and Delta waves during deep sleep. Hypnosis invokes mostly Alpha waves in light trance, and Theta waves during deeper trance, so though alert and responsive to the voice of the hypnotherapist, hypnosis can feel much like a daydream. In this state our inner thoughts and feelings dominate our waking attention, rather than the world "out there".

When in a hypnotic trance, we can easily bring ourselves to full awareness of the outer world whenever there is a pressing need, like a suggestion to do so, or an ordinary interruption like a doorbell, honking horn, or another signal. Without such a signal, it is also possible to bring oneself out of trance as needed.

Hypnosis does not render one powerless.

Together, the client and hypnotist or hypnotherapist enter into a spoken or implied agreement, working as partners in a state of trance, to explore areas of mentation where creativity, imagination or a search for new meaning are the goals. A subject cannot be kept in trance against his or her will.

It is unfortunately true that

hypnotic techniques play a part in the brainwashing of subjects who give their minds over to disreputable or dangerous religious, gang or political leaders - but hypnotic techniques and speech are only portion of their manipulative repertoire. The most manipulative and cult leaders also utilize isolation, fear, rewards and punishments to limit choices of their subjects.

The Relationship between Hypnosis and NLP
NLP was born out of careful observations of therapeutic changes that could happen as a result of good *rapport* and use of hypnotic language between top hypnotherapists and their clients, whether those therapists knew it at the time (Erickson) or not (Perls and Satir). The good therapists were directing their clients to enter a state of trance, in order to diminish current problems or behaviors, and imagine new futures, making them real and compelling enough to pursue.

The hand-in-glove relationship between NLP and hypnosis is an important one, because whatever can be neurologically learned through NLP techniques, can generally be learned more quickly, meaningfully and permanently when in an altered neurological state. In fact, good NLP is always delivered in some kind of altered neurological state, which is experientially distinct from the old habitual state where the old problem was manifest. It has been powerfully demonstrated that when the client can alter their neurological state, entering trance, real and lasting changes can be installed. A skilled hypnotist does not *cause* trance in another person, but rather *leads* a person into a state of trance, which they had always been able to do by themselves anyway, under the right conditions.

Hypnotic Trance is Most Powerful when You Know What You Want

Trance can be a powerful force for healing, learning and integration, or it can be used unproductively as an escape from reality. Likewise, hypnosis can be a powerful ally in forming new beliefs and strategies, or it can be abused as part of a larger campaign to limit our freedoms. And so we see here a potent lesson: understand trance and *know your outcome* before you employ trance as a *resource* for achieving it. Then rely only on reputable hypnotists when pursuing your goals, such as the hypnosis downloads and hypnosis scripts on the following pages:

4. ANCHORING

Anchoring aims to elicit a habitual, positive emotional response to a specific word or physical stimulus. For example, a therapist may be able to induce a patient to smile whenever someone touches their shoulder. This is an extremely powerful way of instantaneously changing the way a person feels, and works well in long term therapist-patient relationships. However, it is also possible to generate these responses yourself, and thus provide yourself with an instant pick-me-up to see you through hard times.

5. BELIEF CHANGE

From childhood onward we gather around ourselves a complex web of beliefs, assumptions and opinions that guide and affect our everyday lives. Many of these are so deeply ingrained that we spend most of our conscious time being completely unaware of them. Some of these beliefs are inherited from the society in which we were formed and others are of our own idiosyncratic creation. We are often unaware of some of these core beliefs until we find them challenged, when we often fly into an otherwise inexplicable defensive rage.

When taken together, an individual's beliefs constitute a person's unique worldview, a web of assumptions whereby we filter and interpret the events going on around us. All beliefs limit our behavior in some way and many have a positive effect. However, some beliefs reinforce negative behavior patterns that have a deleterious effect on the way we think and interact with other people. NLP offers an effective tool set for re-programming your belief set and revising the way you view the world in order to act more positively within it.

In the following series of articles I will examine each of these core NLP techniques in detail and show you how they can be utilized to unlock your latent power to transform your life for the better.

Pace THEN Lead
Pacing **Others**

To get others to willingly follow you, you must *first* have walked in their shoes, and be able to convey that experience to the other. To build *rapport* and relate well, everything begins with pacing another person. Pacing means adopting another person's model of the world, without judgment, and on their terms. This is where the cliché "walking in their shoes" comes from. Once in their shoes, too fast and you'll lose them, too slow and they'll lose you. The onus as a communicator is on you to monitor and keep the pace.

Once you have paced another person, established rapport and shown that you understand where they are coming from, then you have an opportunity to lead them. You intuitively know the moment because when you zig they zig, and when you zag they zag. If you zig and they zag, you there is not enough rapport.

Leading happens only when you use the influence that you have built up from pacing. You cannot lead a another person unless they are willing to be led, and people will not follow unless they have first been sufficiently paced. It works with horses and it works with people.

Pacing Yourself

You also need to pace yourself. Some *spiritual* teachers refer to this experience as becoming present, or getting in touch with your feelings. But in NLP, it is necessary preparation to any significant change.

Pacing is the equivalent of understanding the present *state* in order to build a more appropriate and empowering desired state. For any successful change in yourself or others, pace THEN lead.

Modeling is the basis for NLP, which began with two rebels (Bandler and Grinder) modeling two loners (Erickson and Satir). Then came Dilts, who modeled the likes of Einstein, Sherlock Holmes, Aristotle, Jesus and others.

We can learn a lot from the writings and seminars of these pioneers, but anything we learn from these good people is still 3 steps removed from the original magic they observed.

So there is a great need for ongoing modeling, where we all learn through direct observation of excellence. Here are the basic steps we can all master:

Elicitation

Elicitation is the art of gaining *rapport* with the subject, so that artful questions can reveal the underlying structure of their strategies.

Coding

Coding strategies is identifying and arranging the TOTEs in sequence, using the *submodalities* of the subject.

Installation

Installation is the use of anchors to embed the strategies into our neural networks, so that evoking the *strategy* in real time and in appropriate situations is automatic.

Utilization

Utilization involves both the use of the new strategy in real life, and using feedback to tune up the strategy so that performance and *ecology* are enhanced.

Applications of Strategies

We use strategies in many ways. Here are common strategies that we all have, some of which are more effective than others:
- *Modeling* Success
- Limiting Beliefs
- Learning
- Sales
- Motivation
- Decisions
- Health Habits

TOTEs
NLP *TOTE* **Pattern**
Just like a heat-seaking missile, we can move from any present *state* to another more desirable state or *outcome* by testing for the difference between the two states, moving toward the desired state, test to see if you or closer to or further away from the desired state, and then exit when the desired state is reached.

Present State --> Desired State

Test (for difference) --> **O**peration (take action) --> **T**est (am I there yet?) |- *Yes* --> **E**xit

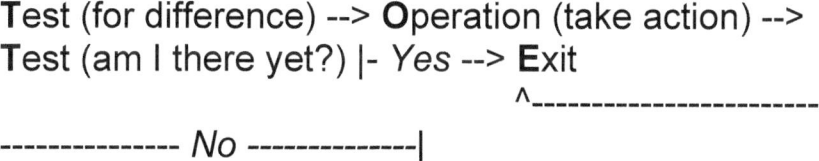

--------------- *No* --------------|

Testing is so important. Ask questions like how will I know I am there? How do I know that I am not there? Without testing or measuring progress toward an outcome, we simply wander aimlessly.

Eliciting Strategies
Eliciting Strategies is a structured process whereby

the sequences of internal and external representations are exposed and documented. It does not matter whether the *strategy* is a desirable or undesirable one.

The Process

You want to take the person into the strategy and make them the expert at what they do.
- Associate the person into the strategy
- Ask to be taken step by step through the strategy
- Distinguish between Sequential and Simultaneous Steps
- Focus on the Process, Not the Use
-

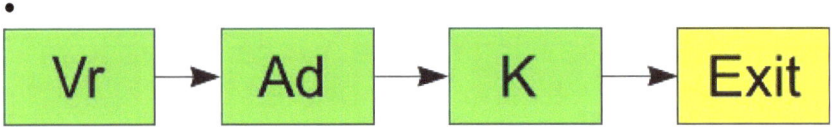

Use *TOTE* Questions

TOTE questions are excellent at keeping you and the person tied to the task of discovering the process and the underlying intent.
- How do you know when to move on?
- How do you transition to next step?
- How do you know when to try something else?
- How do you know when to exit?
- Backtrack often and then ask, Then What?
- Walk through the strategy yourself. Does it make sense?
- Play the strategy back to the person. Does it make sense to them?

Use Submodality Notation

In order to best enter into the world of the person whose strategies you are eliciting pay attention to the *submodalities* in their strategy, note them and

play back the strategies in the submodalities expressed by the person.
- External *Visual*
- Internal Visual Remembered
- Internal Visual Constructed
- Internal Visual *Digital*
-
- External *Auditory*
- Internal Auditory Remembered
- Internal Auditory Constructed
- Internal Auditory Digital
-
- External *Kinesthetic*
- Internal Kinesthetic Remembered
- Internal Kinesthetic Constructive
- Internal Kinesthetic Positive
- Internal Kinesthetic Negative
-
- *Gustatory*
-
- *Olfactory*

Designing Strategies
How are successful strategies custom designed?
Well-defined *Outcome*
It all starts with the end in mind.

Clearly knowing the last step *leading* up to the end of the process is key to achieving the end.
Sequence of Representational Systems - *TOTE* **Operations**
The steps toward the outcome are listed and reinforced so that no question about when one step is complete and the next begins can impede progress.

Critical Submodality Distinctions Determine Exit Point

Installing Strategies

The Two Rules of Installing Strategies

Rule # 1: If it ain't broke, don't fix it!

This rule helps everyone focus on installing strategies that make a positive difference in life. Install strategies that address a presenting problem, or that generate positive improvements in life.

Rule # 2: The new *strategy* must work as automatically as the old strategy

Even a perfect strategy will fail if it does not automatically activate when needed.

Use Anchors to Chain *TOTE*'s together

Anchoring **Process**

- **R**ecall a Vivid Past Experience
- **A**nchor (provide) a stimulus at the peak of the *state*
- **C**hange the state away from the peak state
- **E**voke the anchored state (test)

Keys to Powerful Anchors

- **I**ntensity of the state in which the anchor is provided
- **T**iming of the anchor, or the delivery during the peak of the desired state
- **U**niqueness of the anchor, or the guarantee that it will not fire inadvertently against one's will
- **R**eplicability of the anchor, or the ability to produce it at will
- **N**umber of times the process is repeated. 3, 7 and 21 times seem to be magic numbers.

Collapsing anchors is used to replace a negative anchor with a positive one.

Chaining anchors are used to step a client from a

state of inaction to a state of action, or from a state of overreaction to a state of acceptance.

Test and *Future Pace*
The process of installing a new strategy is not complete unless and until you are sure that the new strategy will kick in automatically and execute flawlessly in a variety of future conditions.

Lather, Rinse, Repeat
To strengthen the new neural networks repetition and repetition in a variety of situations forms a habit.

Emotional States
Emotions. Everybody's got 'em. Not everybody can control 'em... at least not always. They come and go in response to stimuli around us.
But emotional states are more than just emotions. At any moment our state the *sum* of our thinking, physiology and emotions. Our state is greater than the sum of these 3 parts, and taken as a whole is the means for determining the potential of that moment.
One of the most transformational beliefs that one can adopt in NLP is that changing one's emotional state is entirely possible through awareness of one's state, the will to change the state, and knowing how. As soon as one realizes this for the first time, life takes on a vastly new set of possibilities.

Source of Emotions
In NLP, we love to use metaphors to teach important concepts, so that we can leave enough room to allow individual application. Let's use the metaphor of a deep-rooted tree to teach about

emotions, and from whence they arise.

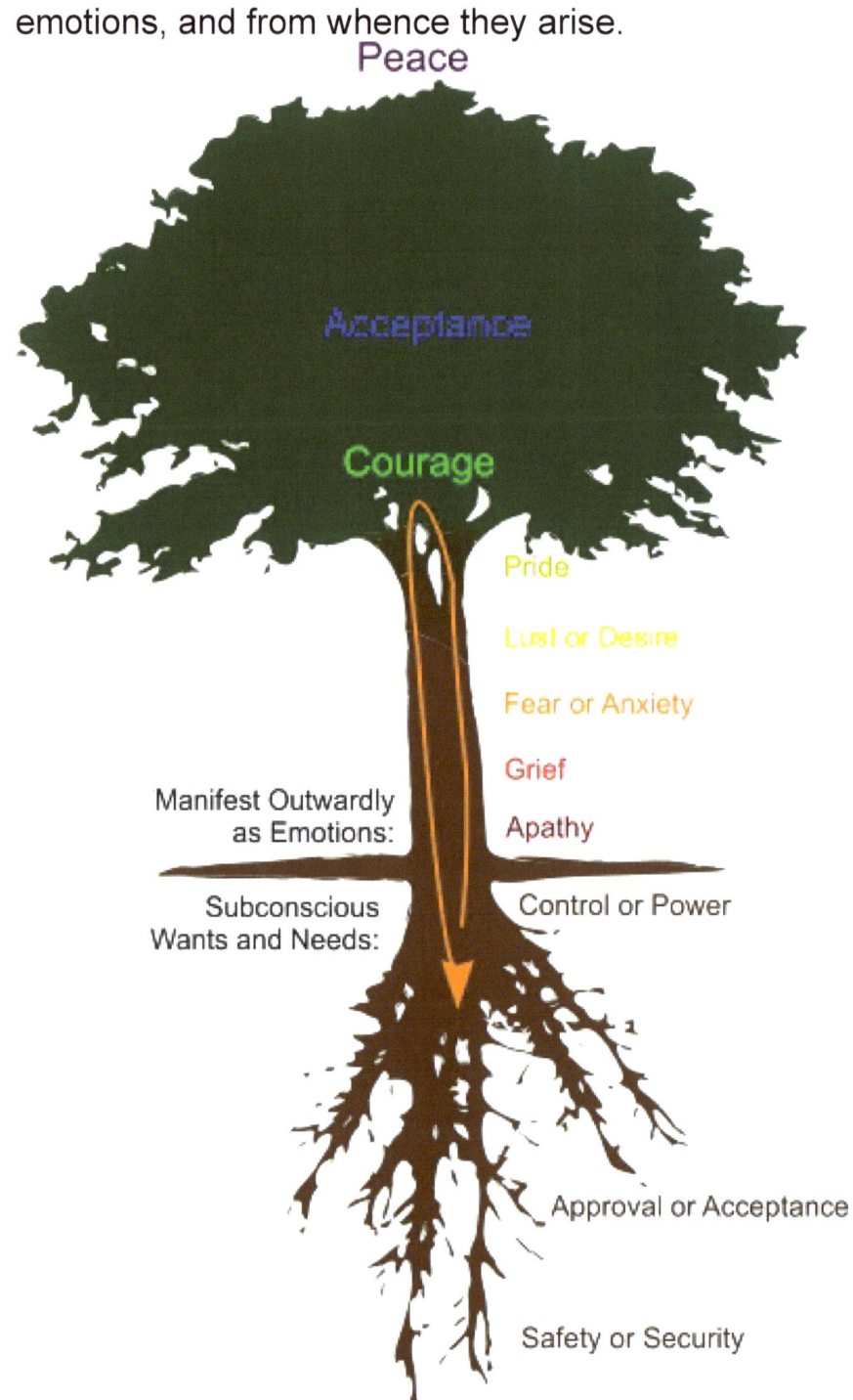

Wants and Needs
Everybody has basic wants and needs, of differing magnitudes, and which are satisfied in different degrees at different times. These basic wants and needs are like appetites, which can only be satisfied temporarily, and then *in time* they require satisfaction again. These basic wants and needs fall in to three general categories:
- Safety or Security
- Approval or Acceptance
- Control or Power

When these invisible wants and needs go unsatisfied, they call on certain emotions to move us in toward sources of satisfaction, or away from sources which would jeopardize that satisfaction.

Emotions
Emotions are "Energy in Motion", and behave like powerful "strange attractors". Each emotion has its own gravity, frequency and energy, and attracts certain recurring thoughts on the same wavelength, and attracts others of the same wavelength, while repelling others on different wavelengths. The gravitational pull of each emotion is so powerful as to attact even circumstances into our lives while we are experiencing these emotions. You might notice how good days have their own momentum, and how bad days have their own inertia. The difference is in the emotion.

Emotions are powerful neurological phenomena, which we inherited from our biology. The bad news is that we cannot escape our emotions. The good news is that we can harness their energy and use emotions to our benefit.

Emotional Circuit

Unfulfilled Wants and Needs > Invoke Emotions > Conjure Thoughts, Images and Words > Result in Outward Expression of Words and Emotions > Impact *Environment*.

If the wants and needs are satisfied, then the circuit is completed, and the energy has completed its course. If the wants and needs are not satisfied, then the energy is blocked, and the wants and needs are intensified.

Fortified with an understanding of this circuit, we can now begin to interact with our emotions in a more resourceful way than ever before.

Ineffective ways to deal with emotions include:
- Ignoring or denying them, which leads to frustration, and eventual emotional eruptions.
- Allowing our emotions to gush upon unwilling audiences, which stresses and damages relationships.

Effective ways of dealing with emotions are:
- Acknowledging them, and giving them a voice, so they can convey to you an unfulfilled need. Thank the emotions for making those needs known to you.
- Recontextualize the stimulus that gave rise to the emotion. Assign a new meaning. Let the emotion be a wise teacher.
- Release the emotion by acknowledge it consciously by welcoming it, diving into it, and then letting it run its course, without causing damage to oneself or others.

Exercises:

Pay attention to your own emotions, and the underlying want or need behind the emotion, which gives it energy.

Is the want or need a strong one, or weak one?

Can you observe that before the emotion arose, the need or want could be detected? How quickly did the need or want make itself known to the emotional center? How quickly did the emotion manifest itself in thoughts or words? How quickly did the emotion manifest itself outwardly, or was it suppressed?

How has applying a new meaning to the stimulus of the emotion been effective in completing the circuit?

How has fully acknowledging the emotion, its underlying need or want, and then simply releasing the emotion completed the circuit?

Negative Emotions

So that we can become better acquainted with our emotions and learn to master them, let's examine the most common emotions, starting with the most negative:

Apathy

Only slightly more energetic than shame, apathy is the emotion with the least amount of life energy. Apathy is the emotion felt during depression. Everyone has bad days, to be sure, but ongoing and severe apathetic episodes can be quite dangerous to one's wealth first, and then health. NLP is not really effective with severely depressed individuals, primarily because of the blocking out of the meaning in language patterns that would otherwise be effective in a person with more energy. For severely depressed individuals, refer them to a healthcare practitioner, then when deemed safe, NLP can be called on to help build a brighter future.

In an apathetic *state*, we feel as though desire is dead and it's no use. We can't do anything, and no one else can help. We feel dense, heavy and see no way out. We withdraw and play weak so we won't get hurt. Our minds can get so noisy that we may go numb. The pictures we have are the most limited and destructive so that we see only failure and how we can't and no one else can, as well. We have little or no energy to act on our pictures and thoughts because inwardly we are being pulled in so many conflicting directions.

It takes quite an initial boost, jolt or shock to move us from this stuck state, and once we manage to break free of apathy, it requires a lot of momentum just to keep from being pulled back in by its powerful gravity.

Here are some of the feelings and words that dominate the thoughts of those in apathy:

- Bored
- Can't win
- Careless
- Cold Futile
- Cut-off
- Dead
- Defeated
- Demoralized
- Depressed
- Desolate
- Despair
- Discouraged
- Disillusioned
- Doomed
- Drained
- Failure

- Forgetful
- Giving up
- Hardened
- Hopeless
- Humorless
- I can't
- I don't care
- I don't count
- Inattentive
- Indecisive
- Indifferent
- Invisible
- It's too late
- Lazy
- Let it wait
- Listless
- Loser
- Lost
- Negative
- Numb
- Overwhelmed
- Powerless
- Resigned
- Shock
- Spaced out
- Stoned
- Stuck
- Too tired
- Unfeeling
- Unfocused
- Useless
- Vague
- Wasted
- What's the use?
- Why try?

- Worthless

Grief

Grieving is a natural process for everyone who experiences a loss. *In time*, most people cycle in and out of grief after the loss, whose severity is a determinant of the length of the process. However, sometimes people are unable to catch the wave out of the depths of grief, in which case they require assistance.

In a state of grief, we want someone else to help us because we feel that we can't do anything on our own, but we hope maybe someone else can. We cry out in pain for someone to do it for us. Our body has a little more energy than in apathy, but it is so contracted that it is painful. Our mind is a little less cluttered than in apathy but still very noisy and opaque. We picture our pain and loss, often getting lost in these pictures. Our thoughts revolve around how much we hurt and what we have lost and if we can get anyone else to help. In most cases, taking the time to adjust to letting go of the loss is the best medicine for grief. The process cannot be rushed, but it can be facilitated by receiving support for day-to-day needs while the healing goes on.

Here are some of the feelings and words that dominate our experience during episodes of grief:

- Abandoned
- Abused
- Accused
- Anguished
- Ashamed
- Betrayed
- Blue
- Cheated
- Despair
- Disappointed
- Distraught
- Embarrassed
- Forgotten
- Guilty
- Heartbroken
- Heartache
- Heartsick
- Helpless
- Hurt
- If only
- Ignored

- Inadequate
- Inconsolable
- It's not fair
- Left out
- Longing
- Loss
- Melancholy
- Misunderstood
- Mourning
- Neglected
- Nobody cares
- Nobody loves me
- Nostalgic
- Passed over
- Pity
- Poor me
- Regret
- Rejected
- Remorse
- Sadness
- Sorrow
- Tearful
- Tormented
- Torn
- Tortured
- Unhappy
- Unloved
- Unwanted
- Vulnerable
- Why me?
- Wounded

Fear

We have the emotion of fear to thank for our existence. Without fear, our ancestors long since would have been killed jumping from high places, drowned in tempestuous oceans, or consumed by stronger and more cunning predators.

Nothing clouds our higher mind quite like fear. In a state of fear, we instinctively strike out, run away or freeze. This is great when the danger is real and immediate, but the problem with fear is that we succumb to it even when the danger is not real, or when it is a low probability, or far away in the future. When experiencing fear, our body has a little more energy than in grief, but it is still so contracted that it is mostly painful. Anxiety attacks can arise out of nowhere. Our mind is a little less cluttered than in grief but still very noisy and opaque. Our pictures and thoughts are about doom and destruction. All we can think and see is how we will get hurt, what we may lose and how we can protect ourselves and those around us.

Here are some of the feelings and words that dominate us during times of fear:

- Anxious
- Apprehensive
- Cautious
- Clammy
- Cowardice
- Defensive
- Distrust
- Doubt
- Dread
- Embarrassed

- Evasive
- Foreboding
- Frantic
- Hesitant
- Horrified
- Hysterical
- Inhibited
- Insecure
- Irrational
- Nausea
- Nervous
- Panic
- Paralyzed
- Paranoid
- Scared
- Secretive
- Shaky
- Shy
- Skeptical
- Stage fright
- Superstitious
- Suspicious
- Tense
- Terrified
- Threatened
- Timid
- Trapped
- Uncertain
- Uneasy
- Vulnerable
- Want to escape
- Wary
- Worry

Lust or Desire

Without the energy of desire, you and I would not be here. Why else would creatures as diverse as a man and a woman otherwise ever decide to get together, unless logic were overridden by desire? Advertisers know well that our economy is powered by desire, so they do their best to link our desires with their products or services. Again, desire is not a bad emotion, but a strong one, that can be tamed and directed in resourceful ways. Untamed, desire can lead to damaged wealth, health and relationships.

In a state of desire, we crave. We hunger for dessert, attention, nicotine, money, power, sex, people, places and things, but there is often a hesitation. We often have an underlying feeling that we cannot or should not have. Our body has a little more energy than in fear. It is still quite contracted, but the sensations now are sometimes quite pleasurable, especially compared to the lower energy emotions. Feelings can be very intense. Our mind is a little less cluttered than in fear but still very noisy and obsessive. We may try and medicate our pictures with positive fantasies, but, underneath, our pictures are really about what we don't have. Our thoughts are about what we need to get and what we don't have. No matter how much we do get, we never feel satisfied and rarely enjoy what we have.

Here are some of the feelings and words that go along with a state of desire:

- Abandon
- Anticipation
- Callous
- Can't wait
- Compulsive
- Craving
- Demanding
- Devious
- Driven
- Envy
- Exploitive
- Fixated

- Frenzy
- Frustrated
- Gluttonous
- Greedy
- Hoarding
- Hunger
- I want
- Impatient
- Lascivious
- Lecherous
- Manipulative
- Miserly
- Must have it
- Never enough
- Never satisfied
- Oblivious
- Obsessed
- Overindulgent
- Possessive
- Predator
- Pushy
- Reckless
- Ruthless
- Scheming
- Selfish
- Voracious
- Wanton
- Wicked

Learn to Use Anchors
Anchors are external triggers the evoke a predictable emotional response in us. Everyone has them... some productive (like not having to think to stop one's car when the light turns red),

and others counter-productive (like that twisted feeling in one's gut when approaching a public speech).

The power in the principle of *anchoring* in NLP is that we can *install* them to manipulate our own *state* from an unresourceful state to a resourceful state at will and as required.

Breaking and Changing States

NLP teaches us that we are responsible (or response-able) for our states. We are empowered to change our states when required or desired. States have a kind of momentum of their own, and so just like a car or a train in motion, we need to know how to engage the controls to make a directional change.

Breaking State

Breaking state could also be thought of as "braking" state. It is a way of interrupting the momentum and energy of a given or induced state. This is done to allow the process to be repeated from beginning to end multiple times during a session, which allows the client to learn to create the state quickly and distinguish the state from what ever state came before.

Changing State

Through the use of anchors, we are able to facilitate the switch from an unresourceful state to a resourceful one.

How To Do An NLP Swish Pattern

This exercise will show you **How to Use the NLP Swish Pattern** – which will help you to act ideally in a situation which is causing you problems at the moment.

If you follow the instructions below, you will discover the cue that makes you act out your undesired response at present – and learn how to replace it with a positive and empowering self image – which will help you to perform at your best. If you're not sure what this means, click on this link to find out more about the NLP Swish Pattern.

NLP Swish Pattern 1: Identify the Problem Behaviour

Before you use the NLP Swish Pattern, you have to know which problem behaviour you are looking to change.

This could be one of the examples listed in my Introduction to NLP Swish Patterns (link above) – such as you don't exercise enough, you eat too much crap – or it could be a fear of meeting new people, of speaking in public, or a fear of failing at any particular endeavour.

All that matters is that it's an *exact behaviour* that you would like to change – to replace with a new positive and empowering response.

Pick a specific problem you are looking to solve with the NLP Swish Pattern before you move on.

NLP Swish Pattern 2: Find The Cue

Your current problem behaviour is likely to be *triggered automatically by a specific stimulus*. This means that you don't consciously choose to act the way you do, you just do. It's an automatic response - just like when the Doctor bangs your knee with a hammer and your leg shoots up.

There is a certain trigger for you that causes you to act out this problem behaviour. If you can identify the trigger, you can change the response with an NLP Swish Pattern.

For example, if you're putting off going to the gym, what is the *exact moment* that you decide not to go? It could be the thought of packing your bag and walking to the gym that makes you decide against it. It might be the mental image of you struggling on the running machine that saps your enthusiasm. It could even be the "better" thought of you lying on the sofa, junk food and TV remote in hand, as a preferred way to spend your afternoon.

Either way, there is a *specific cue* that generates the automatic response. Find this before moving on.

If you're struggling to identify your specific cue, try this little exercise – *imagine that you have to teach me this problem behaviour*.

Imagine that I want to learn how to avoid exercise, or how to eat more crap, or how to be petrified of speaking in public – or whatever your particular issue is.

What is the one image that I would need to picture that would absolutely decide my hand for me? *Which pictures, sounds and feelings* would I have to replicate in my brain to confine me to acting out the undesired response? If you really, truly wanted to convince me why you act the way you do, how would you do so? What do I need to see and feel to make me act this way?

That should've helped you to find your trigger! If you haven't identified your cue yet, simply imagine performing your *desired response* now... what pops into your mind first? How do you manage to convince yourself that this better and more beneficial behaviour is a bad or scary idea?

When you've identified your cue, jot it down on a bit of paper and **break state** – this simply means clearing your brain and doing something else for a few seconds. Jump up and down on the spot, hum a song, recite the alphabet backwards or look out the window for a while... Whatever you fancy. Just think about something totally unrelated for a minute before proceeding. This helps your brain to reset before you go on to identify the new behaviour you wish to install.

NLP Swish Pattern 3: Choose Your Ideal Response

Now we get to the fun part. Here, you get to choose the self image that you will install in your subconscious – the positive response you will generate automatically when the cue occurs from now on.

Choose a suitably compelling snapshot of you performing at your best now – a picture that excites and motivates you.

For example, you might see yourself immediately after a gym session - buzzing on endorphins and feeling wonderful. You might imagine a slim and healthy you who is eating healthily and feeling awesome. It could be a confident and assured you who has just delivered an engaging and well-received presentation to a crowd of strangers and received rapturous applause. Whatever the response you wish to install, get a clear picture of it now.

All that matters is that this response is powerful for *you* – it has to motivate you and you only.

Now... ramp it up! Make the picture big and bright and gorgeously compelling... make the sounds brighter and clearer... and thoroughly indulge yourself in every last glorious detail of this wonderful picture... and make sure you feel exactly how you would feel if you acted in this ideal way in real life... better, in fact.

Now, locate where the feeling in your body is, give this feeling a colour, and double its intensity and brightness... and then double it again! Make yourself feel awesome now by seeing yourself performing at your best – and living it now in the present.

Absolutely wallow in this gorgeous collection of

images, sounds and feelings. Make yourself feel as amazing as you possibly can... and then double the intensity of the feelings again! Make sure your brain is filled with a gloriously bright, crisp and powerful image of you at your best – and feeling on top of the world.

When you've got this wonderful image sorted, **break state**. Count to ten in Japanese. Converse with a pet. Contemplate the nature of the universe... whatever takes your fancy.

NLP Swish Pattern 4: Time To Swish!
This is where the magic happens! What you are going to do is take the original cue image from step 2 and replace it with the new, empowering picture from step 3.

So first, get the old cue picture in your mind. You should be associated – which means seeing it through your own eyes. Make it big and bright and see every little detail.

Now, take a postage-stamp sized picture of your new, powerful self image, and plonk it in the corner of your vision. Make it small and dark and disassociated for the moment – which means looking down at yourself from a third party perspective, not through your own eyes.

Now, we're ready to Swish!

Take the postage sized picture of the new you and push it further and further away from you until it is just a tiny speck. I like to visualise this little picture stretching all the way back to the moon, where I load it with an unimaginably powerful rocket launcher. (In a second we're going to need this image to absolutely fly at you, growing bigger and brighter and more compelling by the millisecond – and I find the best way to do this is by imagining the new picture has a rocket strapped to it. Some people prefer pretending it's on an elastic band – work out what's right for you!)

When you're ready to Swish, fire your rocket or elastic band at full power. As the new image comes hurtling towards you, becoming bigger and richer and bolder – send the old cue image in the opposite direction, armed with its very own rocket launcher, making it darker and smaller and less powerful and flying away from you.

Some people like to make an audible "Swish" sound when they do this – I guess it's the sound you'd imagine these memories to make as they fly past each other.

As the new self image hits you – associate. See it through your own eyes! Imagine every last glorious detail again and make it big and bright and bold and beautiful! Feel all the amazing feelings rush through your veins... And think how good it would be to behave like this from now on.

Take a few moments to revel in the wonderful feeling of this new self image. This is key – indulge yourself. Don't rush this bit... enjoy your success.

Now, **break state**.

NLP Swish Pattern 5: Embed The Change

It's now time to thoroughly embed this change. For the NLP Swish Pattern to work, you need to **repeat the last step 10 times**, breaking state in between each one. You'll find that you'll do this quicker as you progress.

(Don't moan! It will only take you ten minutes tops – and if you've come this far, it's bloody worth it!)

So, load up the old cue image – put the new empowering belief as a speck in the corner – push it back as far as it can go - load it up with your rocket or spring – and Swish! Send the old memory to the moon, and bring the new memory crushing home to you!

Take a few moments between each attempt to *really enjoy the feelings*... you should be having fun when you do this.

To finish, when you have Swished 10 times, think of the cue and then try and think of your old problem behaviour. If you've done it correctly, it will be quite tricky to even imagine the old behaviour – and even if you can, it's most probably lost the majority of its strength. You might even find it a bit funny to imagine yourself behaving in the old way... Success!

You're now left with a new way to act whenever you experience the cue – so enjoy the results from this NLP Swish Pattern!

Changing Personal History

Changing personal history is an NLP intervention that can be done with oneself or with another person. This is a powerful exercise wherein a person (usually in a *trance state*) revisits a traumatic experience of the past, and then through *anchoring*, a bad decision or experience is replaced with a good decision or experience and anchored. Then future *pacing* determines whether this change in the remembered experience is OK.

NLP Techniques and Patterns: Stepping Stones to a New Reality

When we use NLP Techniques, otherwise known as NLP Patterns, or NLP Strategies it is because something is not working in our lives, or not working as well as we would like. We might find ourselves at some kind of impasse, or stuck situation. We want something else, or something better. Then we know to set out to build a bridge from old thoughts, states, feelings, beliefs, or behaviors to new ones. In NLP, we literally build a bridge in our neurology from where we are, to the place we want to be, or from the person we are to the person we want to be come. In NLP jargon, we say that we move from a **P**resent **S**tate to a **D**esired **S**tate, or PS -> DS.

It is the PS -> DS direction that is at the heart of every NLP technique (of which there are at least hundreds). Never forget this formula!

As human beings, we are learning and adapting to changes all the time... We do so very well, in fact. Yet there are all times when we all feel stuck. We need new resources, a new view, a new outlook, a new idea, a token, more information, or advice, motivation or skills, etc. to move us along.

NLP techniques and patterns are simply documented and tested strategies that move us and our human neurology along in a stepwise manner, and in a positive direction.

To use an Engineering *metaphor*, no two bridges are exactly alike, but they all serve the same purpose. Good engineering requires a rigorous study of the terrain, and the load that the bridge must ultimately carry. Real human change engineering is also required when building neurological bridges that will carry the load they must in the future that we want to create.

The NLP bridges we build are all in the mind... which literally updates our neurology or neural networks, as old habits and ways of thinking and feeling are diminished, in favor of new neurological patterns. These new patterns are then reinforced or strengthened until they become habituated, or learned.

How can I learn more about NLP Techniques?
Fortunately, the NLP founders and active NLPers ever since have left a wake of NLP techniques as templates that have stood the test of time, are available online and in books, and new patterns are being modeled all the time by creative NLPers. I highly recommend Shlomo Vaknin's revised edition of The BIG Book of NLP. This book has most of the patterns ever invented and documented, and Shlomo does a great job explaining not only *that* they work, but *how* and *why* they work.

 The Big Book of NLP, Expanded: 350+ Techniques, Patterns & Strategies of Neuro Linguistic Programming

Everyone who lives a number of years, can learn new things, and speak a language has probably used some NLP *strategy* every day of their lives. And how do you know? You know that you are using NLP when what you are doing is *working*! That's the one criteria that permeates every NLP strategy. In NLP, we say that if something is not working, *try something else*!
You can buy the book above, or you can get some

of those techniques here at Grass Roots NLP. We are always adding NLP techniques, patterns and strategies that you can freely use. Credit will be given whenever possible to those who have modeled these patterns originally, but we take liberty, (*and so can you*) of changing those patterns as needed to get the best results.

Where Can I Safely Practice NLP Patterns?
What NLP is all about is building a network of *NLP Practitioners*, who wish to improve their NLP skills in their own lives. One often forgotten aspect of NLP Practitioner is the *practice* that is involved. By consciously practicing strategies that work, these new programs can become *unconscious* and very efficient over time. We also try to make NLP practice as fun and useful as possible, because when it is enjoyable, practice does not feel like work. This is why children learn faster than adults. They do not know that learning is work, and so they do it naturally and unconsciously.

Foundation NLP Patterns
Every bridge needs a strong foundation, and in building bridges to a better future through NLP we need to have a strong foundation of basic NLP patterns.

These NLP patterns are the foundation upon which the rest of the bridge will be built. You will see, hear, and use these patterns over, and over, and over, and over, and over again as you practice more advanced NLP patterns. These are the NLP patterns that touch neurological bedrock, so to speak. *Learn these first*, and *learn them well*. There is no cutting corners.

NLP Techniques: Sensory Acuity
The Idea:
Much of the foundation for all NLP rests on our powers of perception, and on what we do with those perceptions. Light and shadow, rhythms, melodies and harmonies, feelings of all sorts, scents, flavors, textures and contours, figure and ground and movement serve as inputs into our mind, which then filters, distorts, and generalizes minute changes in perceptions as they update the

maps of our minds. The sharper and more trained our perceptions become, the richer the world becomes, while muted or damaged perceptions lead to a very dull, experientially impoverished place.

Our human neurology is a fantastic perceptual instrument tuned and optimized to our world... and the essence of perception lies our ability to *sense change from moment to moment*. If our world did not change from moment to moment, there would be no perception... no news of change to our minds... the vital news that we depend on for all that we notice, for survival, and pleasure.

In NLP, we place a major emphasis on developing ever greater *sensory acuity*, also known as making distinctions, or becoming educated. But good NLP focuses less on academic knowledge, and more on utilizing and sharpening sensory acuity in real time. *It's all about the noticing.* It's about pattern detection, interpretation, and the meaning we make of it. NLP is about noticing something we did not notice before, or that was perhaps not noticed by anyone before. NLP is about paying attention, and lowering our perceptual thresholds to notice more and more... about less and less.

Speaking metaphorically, you can thing about sensory acuity as tuning our neurology to perceive a symphony, where we might only have heard a drone before. Sensory acuity is about tuning our neurology to see perceive explosion of color and movement where there was only a fog before. It's about tuning our neurology to perceive a way through where there was only a wall before.

The Pattern:
1. Tune up your *visual* acuity

Re-acquaint yourself visually with something completely mundane, such as your car dashboard, or the contents of your most cluttered drawer, or with a stock chart, or with your partner. **Do not assign words or meanings to anything you see.**
- Moving your eyes from left to right, notice the way the light falls on every object.
- Notice cast shadows, core shadows, and highlights.
- Notice shapes, outlines and fills.
- Notice ground and figure, or object and space.
- Notice colors and combinations of colors.
- Repeat the exercise, scanning with your eyes from right to left.
- Repeat the exercise, scanning with your eyes from top to bottom.
- Repeat the exercise, scanning with your eyes from bottom to top.

2. Tune up your *auditory* **acuity**

Take some time to dedicate all your attention to your auditory channel in a crowded public place, or in complete solitude. Close your eyes, and begin to pick out discrete sound sources from around you and just notice the following.
- What rhythms can you detect?
- Can you follow slight changes in volume, and range of volume that you can hear.
- Follow along with changes in pitch, and notice any overtones.
- What is the tambor of the sound source? What instrument does it most approximate?
- Notice the direction from your sound source, and any changes in direction. Left and right are pretty easy, followed by front and back, and most difficult is up and down.

- With changes in volume, can you also discern changes in distance?
- With voices, notice any emotion, and how that manifests in terms of the aforementioned *submodalities*.

3. Tune your *kinesthetic* **acuity**

Some people live in their heads, regarding their bodies as transportation for their heads. Other people never know true hunger, and so they are constantly eating, and are never really satisfied. Still other people rely on drugs to bring relief to symptoms they can't quite put their fingers on. Our body speaks to us all the time, yet we don't know how to listen. Take a moment to listen deeply and compassionately to your body. It really is your best friend.

- Notice the first bite of food, compared to the second and the third. Which bite is the one that finally brings satiety or satisfaction?
- Notice where good feelings start and move to, and in which direction and at which speed they may spin.
- Notice where bad feelings start and move to, and in which direction and at which speed they too may spin.
- Notice if you were to interrupt a bad feeling and spin it in another direction, faster and faster, what might happen?
- Notice when you are really fatigued, versus just bored. What are the differences?
- When was the last time you brushed your teeth? Could you sense when your breath might be overpowering someone else before they do?
- Think of someone you trust, and how does your body tell you they are trustworthy?

- Think of someone you could never trust, and how does your body tell you they are not trustworthy?

When to Use This Pattern:

Suffering two bouts of polio, Milton Erickson was dyslexic, color-blind, tone-deaf and confined to a wheelchair during much of his professional life, yet as a hypnotherapist he was able to compensate exquisitely, masterfully and artfully through continuous development of new distinctions in the people he observed. His ability to notice changes in his clients from moment to moment, as well as nuances in in his *environment* were legendary... but he had to work at it.

I suggest that you work on this pattern in all kinds of contexts for the rest of your life. It's in the noticing, that choices are born, and changes can be made.

Credits:

Richard Bandler, John Grinder, and adapted by Craig Pinegar

NLP Techniques: Well-formed Outcome

The Idea:

Good NLP always starts with the question "**what do you want**"? Other disciplines say to "start with the end in mind", and in business, we also say "a problem well-defined is half-solved". If you want something, and you are clear about it, and ferociously committed to achieving it the odds are that you'll be successful in the end. NLP calls this kind of result a *Well-Formed Outcome*, which name came from NLP's linguistic roots. When outcomes are well formed, the journey is also much more enjoyable.

Of all the NLP patterns that exist, this is, perhaps, the *first* pattern to master in your own life, and with your clients. Most other patterns only support the achievement of this one.

The Pattern:

As a *coach*, you will teach the client how to create future outcomes and create powerful motivational links to those outcomes. Your task will be to use good elicitation skills, to help the client become very clear, precise, motivated, and smart about achieving this outcome in the world of real people, and in real time.

1. *State* **the outcome in the positive**
- Use future perfect tense to state the goal: "By June 30, I *will have raised* $6,000 for tuition"
- Avoid the use of negatives in the goal statement. Create a sense of expectancy and anticipation. "Consider it done!"

2. Identify whether you can get this outcome on your own, or only with the buy in of others
- What could you do today, that would move you in the direction of the outcome.

3. Identify When, Where, Who
- You can use a project plan to list the tasks, resources, timeframes, and dependencies, or at least walk through the tasks and write them down on paper.

5. *Chunk* **the steps appropriately**
- The woman who ate the whale did so one bite at a time. Break the tasks in to steps that can be done, measured and evaluated.
- What tasks can you do on a daily or weekly basis that will move you toward your ultimate outcome?

4. Add Sensory-based evidence

- What will you see, hear and feel when your major milestones toward your outcome are acheived?
- What will you see, hear and feel when your outcome is achieved?
- What *behavior* will you display when your outcome is achieved?

You can work on submodality enhancement during this step if the sensory evidence is weak or foggy. "See what you will see, hear what you will hear, speak how you will speak, stand how you will stand".

6. Fortify yourself with the resources you'll need

- Will you require technical competence or skill, Information, cooperation, confidence, communication skill or pursuasion?

You can go inside to elicit whether the client has the resources sufficient for the outcome, and create them if not.

7. Make the goal compelling

- Are you excited to get up every morning and pursue your outcome?
- What obstacles or parts of you create a drag on your motivation?
- What other distractions compete for attention when working on the outcome?

8. Check for *ecology*

- Is your outcome congruent with your own beliefs and values?
- Is your outcome congruent with and supportive of life?

If not, go inside to find out how the outcome can become more ecological.

When To Use This Pattern:

Use this pattern in your own life, and get *really, really* good at it. Since the pattern takes some time to walk through, limit it's use to the really important goals in your life. An hour of planning for a 5-minute task is just not appropriate. But for the really big goals, an hour of planning will go a long way toward achieving your outcome. It is also appropriate on the big goals to review this pattern on a weekly and monthly basis as you progress toward your outcome.

Use this pattern for clients who want an important outcome, but are unclear on how to define that outcome, or how to get started or stay motivated. Use this pattern to teach how to correct course after launching, and how to anticipate navigate obstacles or resource shortfalls.

Credits:
Michael Hall, and others.

NLP Techniques: Pacing and Matching
The Idea:
They say that imitation is the highest form of flattery. When we pace matched the experience of another person, we honor them by joining them in the representation of their world.

Pacing, *matching* and mirroring are ways to gain fast and deep *rapport* with another person. Successful salespeople understand this intuitively. Lovers do this instinctively, and any couple or group with a high degree of camaraderie assume the same postures, gestures, vocabulary, movements and rhythms of others in the group. In an intimate setting rapport can be gained through matching eye movements, postures, breathing, tone, nodding, and other rhythmic gestures.

People can connect by matching with each other at any of the *Neurological Levels*:
- Environmental Matching
- Behavioral Matching
- *Capability* Matching
- Beliefs and Values Matching
- *Identity* Matching
- Sprituality Matching

There are times when it is appropriate to break rapport for the purpose of moving on to another priority. This is most easily and tactfully done by introducing a mismatch into the process.

One of the easiest ways to mismatch is through physiology rather than through words. For example of two people were sitting down and talking and one suddenly stands up. That signals the end of the conversation. More subtle gestures would include leaning away from the person, pointing your feet toward the door, looking at your watch or changing the rate of your breathing and blinking. On the phone, it's also possible to mismatch by changing your tone rate of speed or volume to be much different than that of the person you're talking to. All of these are ways to signal the coming end of a conversation without having to say so directly.

The Pattern:

1. Take on the physiology similar to your partner
- Stand or sit the way your partner is standing or sitting.
- Assume the same posture as your partner
- Assume the same breathing patterns
- Use big or small gestures and rhythms in harmony with your partner
- Match the pitch, quality tone volume and speed

of your partner's voice

2. Match the other person's *representational system* **preferences**
- Compare by *accessing cues* with verbal predicates to determine which representational system your partner prefers
- Does your partner strongly favor one representational system over another?

3. Match the persons met or frames, values, and beliefs
- Use similar words as your partner when speaking about values, believes, standards etc.
- What frames do you discern?
- What emotions are conjured up?

4. Intentionally mismatch your partner
- Intentionally mismatch one or more of the elements you were matching earlier, and observe just how quickly rapport can evaporate.

5. Regain rapport through matching
Repeat steps 1 through 3, until rapport is again established.

When To Use This Pattern:
Use this pattern in conjunction with all other NLP patterns. Good NLP requires a *state* of rapport between client and *coach*. If rapport is ever lost during an NLP pattern, stop and regain rapport before continuing.

Use this pattern in your romantic endeavors, in your profession, and with family and friends, and notice how life's skids are greased just a little more.

Credits:
Michael Hall, and others.

NLP Techniques: State Calibration

The Idea:
In NLP, "*calibration*" refers to using our *sensory acuity* to guage the mental and emotional *state* or mood of a person or audience. This ability sharpens with experience, and is a critical factor in the success of any NLP intervention, because when delivering a pattern, *timing is everything*. There are many individual clues that our body gives off to reveal one's inner state at any time, including eye access cues, breathing patterns, perspiration, skin tone and color, not to mention posture, voice tone, hesitation in answering, etc. Each of these can be a study unto itself, but a seasoned NLP practitioner will take all of these cues together as a set and then identify areas of *incongruence* or inconsistency.

Not all signals from another person are of equal importance. What is most important in calibration is that you know if you are getting a positive (+) or negative (-) response. Yes means, I'm with you, please continue, this is working. No means, I'm resisting this, there is something you are missing, this is not working.

Besides calibrating a Yes or No response, here are some other kinds of Positive or Negative responses you can *calibrate*:

Calibrating Like vs. Dislike
- Ice Cream
- Cold Showers
- Deserts
- Waiting in Line

Friend vs. Foe
- Hitler
- Bush
- Gandhi

- Santa Claus

Interesting vs. Non-interesting
- Seinfeld
- Animal Planet
- Discovery Channel
- ESPN

The Pattern:

In this pattern, we will simply calibrate the yes/no response of a partner, first verbally, and then non-verbally. Then switch.

1. Practice calibrating verbal yes/no responses

Ask 10 - 20 light questions, and be sure to keep them light. Choose questions whose yes/no answers will be spontaneous and quick.
- Is your name Susan?
- Do you drive a Ford?
- Did you go to Oxford?
- Have you ever been skiing?
- Have you been skiing recently?
- ...

2. Note physiological responses to verbal yes/no responses

During the elicitation, make mental notes of physiological shifts that occur concomitant to a yes or no.
- Is there nodding or a head tilt?
- Is there a change in eye pupil dilation or eye direction?
- Is there eye contact avoidance or excess eye contact with a response?
- Is there a shift in face or neck color?
- Do the hands activate in response to a yes or no?
- Does breathing rate change with a yes or no response?

- Does breathing in the stomach or chest change with a yes or no response?
- Does the body lean forward or back with a yes or no?
- What else can you consistently recognize?

3. Practice calibrating non-verbal yes/no responses

Now, repeat the 10 - 20 questions, or come up with a new set. This time, however, request that your partner only *think* of the yes or no response, but that they do not say yes or no aloud. Write down the yes or no response next to your question, and see how many you guess correct.

4. Rotate

If you are playing this as a game, then switch partners and repeat.

When To Use This Pattern:

Try this pattern at home, in your relationships, with your co-workers and clients. You do not need to announce that you are playing a game with them, but you will come to know when you are in agreement or disagreement regardless of what is being said outwardly.

Credits:

Michael Hall, and others.

NLP Techniques: Checking Ecology

The Idea:

In doing change work that is NLP, it is critical before implementing any change that the change itself be ecological. We like to say don't fix what ain't broken. This is true in NLP and is common sense in life. Making a change can end up to be disastrous if we don't take time to step back and evaluate the impact of the change before making it.

So in NLP we stress ecological checks before installing any new program.

An ecological check means stepping back from the proposed change to think about it in a disassociated way. We evaluate the future as though the change were made to see if there are any negative, harmful, or unnecessarily expensive results caused by its implementation. This gives us an opportunity to debug the new program before it is ever installed.

Whenever we engineer anything for human use, whether it be a new bridge, new biotechnology, a new software system, it is critical that we perform the necessary functional and stress testing before we put that new program into production. Neuro-linguistic programming is no different. We check to make sure that the program performs the desired function in the desired *context*, and it that it performs well.

A simple neuro-linguistic program that is designed to solve a specific persistent problem, such as allergies, can be tested against the introduction of an allergen, and then you'll know whether program will stand up in real life. In contrast, a more complex neuro-linguistic program that is designed to help someone change it deep-seated metaprogram requires more thorough testing in more contexts and more possible kinds of stresses before that program can be six should be installed. For example, moving from a victim mentality to an absolutely confident mentality needs to be tested in a variety of contexts where confidence will be required.

As we debug the new neuro-linguistic program we check for certain things:

- **Conflicting Outcomes**: Does this program interfere with other programs?
- **Loss of Present Benefit**: Does the new program take away any currently available choices?
- **Bad Fit**: Does this program address the presenting problem or goal, or something else?
- *Incongruence* **within the Person Making the Change**; Is there any part within the person that disagrees or may sabotage the new program?
- **Possible New Problems**: Does the new program create new problems which significantly offset the new gains?
- **Unfulfilled Needs**: are there any other gains to be had which are not addressed in the new program?

The Pattern:

1. Invite the person to take a step back
- Think about the new program in the future in a disassociated way
- As you think about the new program, feeling, *state*, *belief* or decision, is it ecological?
- As you think about the new program, do you feel that it is life enhancing?

2. Invite a higher level evaluation
- As you implement this new choice, will it serve you well?
- Does every part of you find it useful?

- Is there any part of you that would object to it?
- What are the new choices or limitations brought about by this new way of being or operating?

3. Step back further to evaluate your criteria for checking ecology
- What standards do you use to make this evaluation?
- Are the standards suitable for the kind of change you want to make?
- Are the criteria of your standards properly weighted?

4. Explore the Cartesian Coordinates
- If I make this change, what will happen?
- If I make this change, what won't happen?
- If I don't make this change, what will happen?
- If I don't make this change, what won't happen?

When to Use This Pattern:
Use this pattern in all kinds of change in your life and with clients. Use this in project planning, software engineering, organizational engineering, and human engineering. Good NLP patterns ALWAYS include ecology check. If any program proves to be un-ecological, stop while you are in the development phase and modify the program before you install it.

Credits:
Richard Bandler, John Grinder, Michael Hall, and others.

NLP Techniques: Flexible Response
The Idea:
There are certainly times when the same old response is appropriate. However, having more choices in a dynamic world is generally desirable, and very often highly prized. In NLP we

presuppose that the meaning of our communication is the response we get. More often than not the intention economy and what we say will be understood somewhat differently than we intended it. So we often need multiple ways of saying or doing something in order to get a response that we want. If we keep trying the same thing over and over, and harder and harder, we can only expect the same results.

In NLP is critical that we operate out of the other person's model the world. That model of the world is only made known to us in bits and pieces as we are able to discern other world is represented in their model. Our understanding of another person's model improves with experience with the person. The person's model of the world shifts over time, as do the moods and states of the person we are working with. What works one day may not work the next. So because NLP is results-oriented, we need to be able to quickly shift our approach to match the current model moods and states of the person we are working with.

Our models of the world are gained through osmosis, since before birth. Even in utero, our neurology is taking in the information about the world and organizing it in terms of what is friendly, and what is dangerous. Through our years we subconsciously come to learn who we can trust or not. On through adolescence, our *belief* systems are forming, and all of this external input comes to form our internal map. The trouble is most people fail to ever recognize the difference between their internal map of the world and the real world on the outside. We come to confuse our beliefs with facts, and never question those beliefs. When beliefs are to longer questioned, then learning and change become retarded or stopped. The more we question our beliefs, or can guide another to do the same, the more we are able to recognize them as mental constructs only, which then allows us to develop richer *flexibility* in the world.

The Pattern:

1. Identify areas in your life where more flexibility would be an asset
- Where are you or your client feeling rigid, stuck or limited?
- Where do you feel you are cycling through the same old routines, unable to escape?
- Does your approach feel rigid anyway?

2. Take a step back and look at the situation in a disassociated way
- From a disassociated perspective what choices do you see yourself having in that situation?
- From that disassociated perspective, what choices would other sage advisers give you?
- If you could not be fired for what you really want to say, what would you say?
- What choices are available within your *unconscious* mind?

3. Make contact with the states that support that flexibility
- Can you sit or stand, or move your eyes in a way that allows more creativity to flow?
- Can you remember a time when your wit and imagination were unstoppable? Can you recall those feelings now?
- Are there *leading* words that you can use that would *elicit* a more flexible response, such as "let's rewind...", or I'm curious...", or "how would it work if..."?

When to Use This Pattern:
Just like a good stretch every morning helps your body to stay toned and fit, stretching your flexibility and responses are useful skill to have in everyday life, but especially in NLP work when going for a particular *outcome*. Try to be flexible in your romantic endeavors, *not* to gain dominance over your partner, but to keep things interesting and exciting. Try saying something in a brand-new way. Remember that the response you get will tell you whether the way you said it comes across to your partner the way you intended it. Keep trying new ways when saying I love you, or discussing chores, or telling about your day at work. Pay attention to accuse your partner is giving you at all times.

If you are in a sales job, and your prospect is looking at his watch, you have to try something new and fast. Watch for cues to determine whether what you are saying is moving them to closer or further away from the close.

In talking to yourself, try talking in a new tone of voice or from another perspective, while paying attention to the other signals you get in your mind and body, to see if the new way of talking motivates you in a stronger way.

Credits:
Michael Hall, and others.

NLP Techniques: State Elicitation
The Idea:
State Elicitation is one of the core skills of any NLP *coach*. In NLP, a state is more than I thought. A state involves thoughts, feelings and physiology, and covers the spectrum from deep relaxation to to high excitement, from acute pain to ecstatic

pleasure, or from mental vertigo to flow. A good NLP practitioner needs to be able to "light up" the neurology, in order to disassociate an old state from an undesirable *outcome*, or to associate a new resourceful state to a new desired outcome. Good neuro-linguistic programming does not happen through intellectual discussions about change. Real change only happens as a result of installing a new neuro-linguistic program in a receptive state. The new neurolinguistic program must be powerfully linked to resourceful states, just as any old unresourceful states must be de-linked. NLP must be experienced, not merely thought about. The role of a good NLP practitioner is to teach the client that they have choices about their states, and that they can enter resourceful states as required. Again, this teaching does not happen through discussion only, but through directly experiencing changes in states.

Here are some states that you may wish to evoke in yourself or client when you wish to move away from some compulsive *behavior*:
- Anger
- Disgust
- Fear

Here are some transitional or interruptive states that you may wish to evoke in yourself or client in order to interrupt an old program, and prepare for new learning:
- Disarray
- Confusion
- Shock

And here are some resourceful states to which we would *anchor* new positive behaviors:
- Peace

- Joy
- Forgiveness
- Willingness
- Courage
- Focus
- Going for It

The Pattern:

1. Bring yourself to an *uptime* state
- Open up all your input channels including your site your hearing and your feelings in the present moment.
- Become acutely aware of the signals being sent out by the person in front of you.

2. Assist the person in accessing the state
- Think of a time when you felt _____, and give it a name.
- What would it be like if you were thinking or feeling _____, right now?
- Do you know anyone who thinks or feels _____?

3. Clarify the essential aspects of the state
- What about this state captures the essence of it for you?
- What about this state makes it distinct from all other states for you?
- Avoid emotionally or semantically loaded references.

4. Elicit the state in a congruent and precise manner
- Carefully choose your questions, and support those questions with voice tone and *body language* congruent with the question.

5. Give the elicited state time and space to emerge
- Remain comfortably in silence while the elicited

state forms and expresses itself.
- Comfortably reward small steps in the right direction, using confirmations such as "that's right", "there you go", etc.
- If the client responds with "I can't", then encourage them to act *as if* it were possible, and "what would that state be like"?

6. Use vague language patterns in order to elicit a trans-derivational search
- Integrate commands such as "just think about", "you know", "try to understand", "could you teach me", "can you remember", "try to experience", "just notice", "become aware", in order to encourage the client to go inside and search their experience.

7. Watch and listen for and match the person's predicates
- Remain in tune with the person while listening for sensory predicates, such as seeing, hearing, or feeling parts of the state you are eliciting.
- When eliciting a past state, encourage the person to see what they saw, hear what they heard, and feel what they felt.
- When eliciting a hypothetical state, encourage the person to see what they would see, hear what they would hear, and feel what they would feel.

8. Use good *downtime* suggestions to light up the neurology
- Help the person go deeper inside to more fully experience the state in their neurology.
- You can just feel those feelings again now, can't you?
- You can just make the picture older and brighter, while you make the sound deeper, and the

flow of emotion more powerful, can't you?
- Now you can double the sensation, and double it again!

When to Use This Pattern:
Use State Elicitation as part of almost any NLP intervention. Remember that it is an art, and not a science. Pay attention to the person in front of you as you ask for the state to come out!
Many persistent problems in relationships are caused by one or both partners becoming stuck in an un-resourceful state, *leading* to more and more problems caused by acting out of that state. With courage and skill the partners can learn that states can be changed rapidly and effectively, allowing better outcomes to flow out of that state. It is important to be able to go into a learning state when studying, a relaxed state at the end of the day, a pumped up state just before working out, a friendly state when meeting with the new client, a rational state when being sold, or a light *trance* when integrating new learnings.
Founders of NLP often asked "who is driving the bus", implying that each of us is responsible for controlling and directing our own states.

Credits:
Michael Hall, and others.

NLP Techniques: State Induction
The Idea:
State Inductions are used when an NLP *coach* wants to produce a neuro-chemical shift in the body-mind of the client. There are simply certain neurological states in which we get our best results. For example, there are times when we need to learn something, focus or concentrate on

performing a complex task, relax or forgive someone, or get amped up and motivated for action. In these neurological states, excellence becomes possible.

In NLP, states are neurological conditions with distinct brain waves and chemistry at work. We can invoke or induce these states at will, if we only know how.

There are 3 common ways we access desired states to create them in ourselves:
- Remembering a time in the past when we experienced the state strongly
- Using imagination to create a fresh experience of the state in the present
- Catching that state from someone else who does it well (to get crazy, think of your favorite Jim Carrey movie)

States come and go all the time, like waves in the ocean. We are constantly shifting between states, and each state swells and ebbs like a wave. Sometimes states are experienced as distinct, and sometimes two or more states can co-exist, and amplify or cancel the effect of the others.

Remember that in NLP, we want to *anchor behavior* to resourceful states, so we must be able to induce the desired state and anchor the new behavior at the very peak of that state.

A master at inducing positive states in thousands of people at once is Tony Robbins. You may have heard help pumping up a crowd with shouts of "yes" and "aye". It really works, if you know how.

The Pattern:

1. Be ready to catch the induced state as it occurs and anchor it when it peaks

Like a surfer trying to catch a good wave, be ready

to watch for the induced state and anchor it with your client. Stay in the present. Stay in up-time awareness. You are outwardly focused on the physiology of your client. You are teaching the client how to do this for his or herself.

2. *Elicit* **a time when the client felt the state strongly in the past**

For this elicitation, remember to ask the questions briefly, and take the first response. Do not dwell on any one question too much. Watch for a physiological shift.

- Recall a time when you felt _____.
- Go back to that experience and see what you saw, hear what you heard, and feel what you felt.
- Notice exactly what was going on inside of yourself at that time.
- Notice the energy as it starts in one place and moves through your body.
- Where does the feeling start, where does it end, and which direction does it rotate?
- What color would you give this feeling?
- Are you there yet? Good.

3. Amplify the intensity of the elicited state

When you start to notice a physiological shift, you know you have accessed the state. Now to make the state stronger and more distinct. Here are some ways to amplify high-energy states:

- Now, double the brightness and sharpness. Add more color.
- Now, double the volume and the bass.
- Now, double the feeling as it flows through you in a circuit.
- Double the speed of the feeling as it flows through you. Now, double it again.

Here are some ways to amplify states of relaxation and learning:
- Now, soften the brightness and deepen the colors.
- Now, diminish the volume to a very relaxing level.
- Now, unwind the tension and continue to allow it to unwind.
- Now, take those feelings of relaxation and double them, double the relaxation again.

4. Access the physiology of the amplified state

Remember that physiology is an important part of any state, and should be congruent with the inner state you are trying to induce. The mind and body should be on the same wavelength.
- When accessing high energy states, the client should be standing, *pacing* or leaning forward in the chair, ready to pounce. Breathing should be higher in the chest, and the pulse should be elevated.
- When accessing relaxation or learning, the client can be comfortably seated with breathing lower in the stomach. Soft eyes. Soft face. Everything is OK.
- **5.** *Calibrate* **the state**

Ask the client to report the amplified state, and contrast it with the originally induced state.
- How motivated or relaxed do you feel now, on a scale from 1 to 10? (e.g., 4)
- How motivated or relaxed did you feel when we started, on a scale from 1 to 10? (e.g., 9)
- How did you get from 4 to 9?

6. *Break state* **and repeat**

Repeat the example steps 2 through 5 up to 3 times, each time getting faster and faster at accessing the new resourceful state.

When To Use This Pattern:
Use State Induction patterns when inducing a resourceful state that you want to anchor in yourself or in a client.
Credits:
Richard Bandler, Tony Robbins, Michael Hall, and others.

NLP Techniques: Break State
The Idea:
Breaking *State*, or applying a Break State is useful for times in life and in NLP work when we simply need to say "STOP!" because the present state is taking us nowhere, or in the wrong direction.

A *Break State* pattern is also used often to build repetition into an NLP intervention, where the client will learn by repeatedly getting into and out of a state. A Break State provides that repetition. And sometimes saying "stop" to an inappropriate state will work, but often not, because most states have a momentum of their own... like a flywheel on an engine. When is the last time you tried to ask a child to stop crying, or a person with depression to stop feeling that way? Were the results good?

So when we want to interrupt an unresourceful state in our selves or in a client, we need better tools. The best tools have an element of surprise, shock or unusualness to them. A child will almost always stop their crying if candy is presented to them out of the corner of their eye. Hearing a coin hit the ground will cause most people to pay attention if only for a second or two. Good humor is based on some kind of surprise in an otherwise predictable stream of words or circumstances.

Pattern interrupts or state breaks happen naturally around us all the time. Whenever we notice a very attractive person, or a very ugly person, even if we look at them through our peripheral vision, they captivate our attention. Seeing a bald eagle, or a fighter jet in the sky will distract most people, and so would the sound of screeching tires.

Notice as you go through the day how many times state interrupts occur, and then pay attention to what happens *next*. Do you go back to the previous state, or are you on to a different one entirely?

The Pattern:

1. Name the current state
- Welcome your mood, state of mind and emotions? What are they saying? What state are you in now?

2. Introduce some surprise into the state, focusing on the *submodalities* that matter most
- What are the modalities of the current state? *Visual*? *Auditory*? *Kinesthetic*?
- What are the visual submodalities, i.e. brightness, color, size, and distance?
- What are the auditory submodalities, i.e. volume, direction, timbre, and tone?
- What are the submodalities, i.e. locus of feeling, positive or negative, speed, and direction?

3. Deliver the interrupt
- Do something sudden and very unusual, and for maximum effect, play on the submodalities from the prior step.
- If a person's problems are "looming large" interrupt by pointing to that flock of birds in the far distance.
- If a person's inner voice is negative and anemic, interrupt by mimicking Jim Carrey saying "AAAAALRIGHTY THEN!!!!!!"
- If a person is feeling a weight in the chest, interrupt by deeply gasping in surprise at something going on behind them, even if it was nothing special.
- For less dramatic effect, you could simply motion a "T" with your hands for a time out, or motion with your hand to wipe clear an imaginary screen.
- You might also just raise or lower your voice by an octave, or speak in a sexy tone or an accent from some other country.
- A famous NLP verbal interrupt that is also subtle and works in most situations is to ask, "do you smell popcorn?"

When To Use This Pattern:

Use a Break State pattern whenever you need to to jar or deliver a mild shock to your consciousness or that of a client. When the conscious mind is momentarily distracted and trying to make sense of the surprise, can a new pattern be introduced. Pattern interrupts can also be delivered during an NLP intervention, while repeating shifts from one state to another. This repetition trains the client to be able to interrupt themselves on cue, and move to the new, more resourceful state.

Credits:
Richard Bandler, John Grinder, Michael Hall, and others.

NLP Techniques: Anchoring

The Idea:

In NLP, the process of *anchoring* is central to producing permanent change. We owe a debt to Ivan Pavlov, for making famous the notion that stimuli can lead to a certain behavioral response. Pavlov took dogs in a *state* of hunger, and rang a bell just before spraying meat powder into the dogs' mouths. After a few rounds, the dogs began to salivate at the sound even when there was no meat powder. NLP takes conditioning into the real human world, however. In NLP, an *anchor* is a certain precise stimulus delivered in a peak emotional state to link powerfully to an underlying meaning within our neurology.

Think of an anchor as a button that can be pushed by oneself or someone else any time we desire a certain response. Think of a certain voice that when you hear it can make your blood pressure rise. Think of a song that makes you remember your high school days. Think of a food that send you running to the bathroom. Think of the perfume reminds you of your first romance. These are all anchors, powerfully linked to a neurological meaning. These are the buttons. Once installed, those buttons are always available to be pushed. In order to uninstall an old button, or install a new button, we must be in a peak emotional state at the time, and at that moment the underlying meaning to which the button is linked must also be evoked. When we choose an anchor to install, there are four characteristics that make that anchor a good

choice:
- **Intensity**: intensity of the feelings of the state at the time of being anchored
- **Purity**: the distinctiveness of the state being anchored
- **Uniqueness**: the more unusual the anchor, the less light leak it is to be pushed by accident
- **Timing**: install the anchor when a person's state reaches its peak

The mnemonic of IPUT, can help you member these qualities.

The Pattern:

1. Identify behavior, state, or response you want to access in the future, and a suitable anchor
- What is the behavior or state you want to be able to produce on demand?
- What kind of an anchor could we use that is obvious to you but discrete to everyone else?

2. *Elicit* **the desired state**
- Invite the person to remember, imagined, or think about the desired state, and experience it fully, now.
- Determine whether the person can make the state intense enough on their own to anchor it successfully.

3. *Calibrate* **the person in the state, and amplify it**
- What are you feeling now?

- What are the unique qualities of this state?
- Now take those feelings and double them, and double them again!
- Make the pictures bolder, brighter and closer!
- Make this sounds louder, clearer and in stereophonic surroundsound!
- Take the good feeling and spin it faster and faster!
- Now stand and breathe confidently!

4. Install the anchor
- Once the person has reached a peak state, and you can easily discern it I calibrate a make the noise, say the word, touch the arm, or make a face that will serve as the anchor in the future. Remember intensity, purity, uniqueness and timing.

5. *Break state* **and test the anchor**
- ask, which we did you drive to get here this morning? Nice weather today, isn't it?
- Now, what happens when I do this: (fire off the anchor).
- When the anchor was fired, did you get the desired response? If yes, you're ready to test in the real world. If no, repeat steps two through four.

When To Use This Pattern:
In your life you can using anchoring to reinforce excellent behavior. Whenever you catch yourself doing something great, amplify the great feelings and then fire off an anchor that you previously selected for its purity and uniqueness. This action will associate the anchor with the neurological meaning underlying those great feelings. Then, in the future when you need to access this state again, you can fire the anchor and it will be there

for you.

Use the Anchoring pattern with your clients, during interventions when new state-dependent behaviors are being installed. This works great in relationships, when seeing their partners should evoke a good feeling. Having an anchor associated to a good feeling can put your client in a good state in a flash, whenever he or she needs it.

Credits:
Richard Bandler, John Grinder, Michael Hall, and others.

NLP Techniques: Positive Intent
The Idea:
In NLP, there is a powerful presupposition that at some level, every *behavior* has some positive intent behind it... even those behaviors that seem negative. Though many people outside of NLP might disagree philosophically with this presupposition, we stand by its power to deliver great results in change work, or in an arbitration setting between two parties. As we address problematic emotions and behaviors, we assume that they serve or have served some useful purpose, and so by learning what that positive intent is or was, we can find a better substitute motion or behavior that delivers that same intent. In order to replace a negative emotion or behavior with a more positive one, we must first give it an audience, hear and honor it for its positive intent, and ask its permission to do something else instead. Once the positive intent is satisfied, then the negative emotion or behavior is no longer required in order to achieve it.

The Pattern:

1. Identify and negative emotion or negative behavior
- What is the problem or trouble that seems to serve no useful purpose for you?
- What difficulties do you struggle with that seem to be negatively motivated?
- Is there a part of you that makes you act selfishly, hesitantly, brashly, irresponsibly?

2. Find the part responsible for the negative behavior, and address it directly
(Remember that there are really no "parts", but there are aspects of our personalities that we can address as though they were distinct parts.)
- Close your eyes and go inside yourself, and get in touch with the part of you that causes you to behave that way.
- Ask that part, what is the positive reason or intent for that behavior?
- Ask that part, what other positive reasons or intentions might there be?

3. Ask questions that *chunk* **up on a** *positive intention* **until you arrive at a level where new agreement can be made**
- When that part of you gets what it wants for you, what does that get you?
- And when you get that, then what does that get for you?
- And when you get that, is the intention fully satisfied?

4. Ask permission of that part to find a new way to achieve that highest intent
- Is it okay now for your *unconscious* mind to find a new way to achieve that intent?
- Are there any aspects of that part of you that might not allow you to find a new way to

> achieve your intent?
- Is there any other part of you that objects to finding a new way to achieving that intent?

When To Use This Pattern:

Use this pattern in your own life when trying to replace that nagging voice in your head with another voice is more soothing, encouraging and positive. Use this pattern to understand the positive intent of others who might have ignored, shamed, or otherwise harmed or hurt you. This does necessarily mean that those who might have gravely harmed you should not be prosecuted, but it will help your unconscious mind to reach a place of understanding, *leading* to forgiveness, so that you can move on with your life.

Use the Positive Intent pattern with your clients to help them understand that it's okay to find better ways to achieve a positive *outcome*. This pattern is great for diminishing guilt, self derision, and for helping to repair or improve relationships.

Use the Positive Intent pattern in negotiations when two parties cannot agree on the details, but may agree by chunking up to a higher level.

The Positive Intent pattern also works great with kids and teenagers, and is a life skill to be developed early and often.

Credits:

Michael Hall, and others.

Wholeness NLP Patterns
NLP Techniques: Keeping It Together

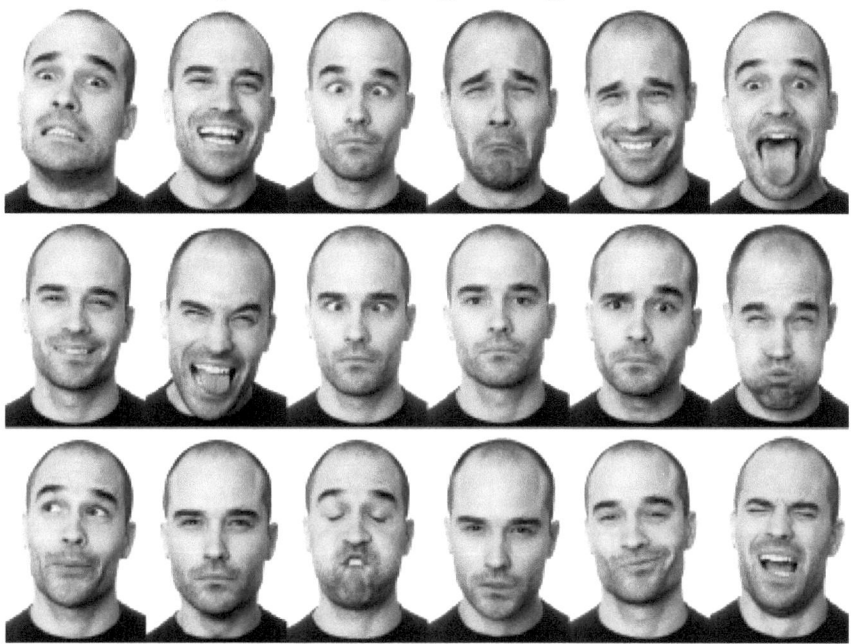

This section is dedicated to NLP Techniques and Patterns for helping us become more congruent and whole.

Not only do we sometimes have disagreements with others, but we also have disagreements with ourselves at certain times, and around certain topics, issues and desires. We can't seem to get any momentum on the things we really want. We spin our wheels in one place, unable to get ourselves unstuck.

Say hello to our "parts". Our parts are purely fictional, facets of our whole person, or more specifically, part of our emotional mind-body system. Still, "parts" are a useful *metaphor* that we easily understand, and commonly refer to in everyday conversations, such as:

- There is a part of me that wants to tell him what I think, **but** another part of me that wants to avoid the issue.
- There is a part of me that needs freedom, **but** another part of me that says wait for a better time!
- I want to go to the gym, **but** that nagging voice on my head keeps reminding me of all the work at the office.

Sound familiar? Did you notice all the "**buts**"? If you count more than a few buts in your own language, it's probably time to look inside for the incongruencies, so they can be heard, respected, and brought to agreement.

NLP Has Some Good News...

The good news is that it is also easier to resolve conflicting parts with NLP Techniques than you might think. When all of our "parts" are recruited, enrolled in support of a common motivation, and not stepping all over each other, life suddenly becomes easy. The following NLP patterns will help you find *congruence* in yourself, and make your life more whole:

NLP Techniques: Collapsing Anchors
The Idea:

You remember *anchoring* from the foundational NLP patterns, and now it's time to learn how to set two anchors (a negative and positive anchor) on a collision course with each other in order for the positive anchor to cancel out the negative one. The Collapsing Anchors pattern is useful when we observe two radically different states operating within us at the same time, interrupting each other, interfering with each other, or even worse, creating

self-sabotage. Examples of opposing states would be:
- Feeling happy, while feeling anxious
- Feeling motivation, while feeling hesitation
- Feeling attraction, while feeling fear

Crashing these two opposing states into each other within the neurology creates a strange starburst of a reaction, resulting in temporary confusion, disorientation, or even light amnesia, after which the force of the negative state is consumed and digested by the positive state.

Personally I don't like the name "collapsing anchors", as much as I like to think of this pattern as negative state annihilation, because I think this is what's really happening inside neurology. Whatever you call this pattern (others call it "integrating anchors"), it really works, but don't try it until you first master setting anchors one at a time.

The Pattern:

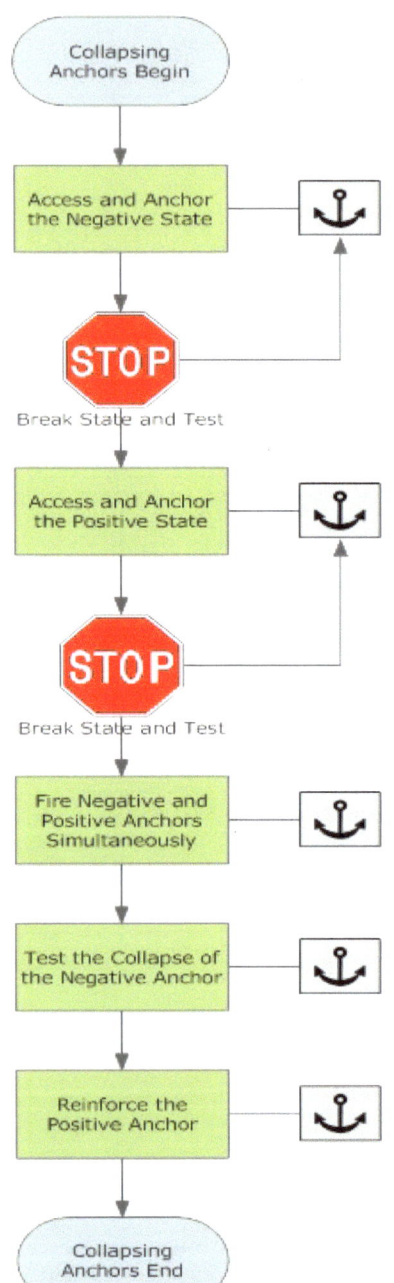

1. Access and anchor the negative state
- What state do you get into often that interferes or interrupt you when you're involved in something important or critical?
- What buttons do you have that you find others pushing?
- Access that state right now... go into it now and see what you see, hear what you hear, and feel what you feel when you're at the height of the state.
- When you're feeling that completely, now, I'm going to touch you right here (touch the left knee or left palm).
- Test the negative anchor and *calibrate* the negative state.

2. *Break state*
- Is that smoke on the horizon? Naw, maybe that's just a cloud.

3. Access and anchor the positive state
- Now, what would you like to experience in that situation?
- See what you'll see, hear what you'll hear, feel what you'll feel when you're in that resourceful state fully.
- Now take that feeling and double it... spin it faster... make the colors bolder, and the picture larger. Add your favorite rock music to the feeling, and turn it up!
- When you're feeling that completely, now, I'm going to touch you right here (touch the right knee or the right palm).
- Test the positive anchor and calibrate the positive state.

4. Break state again

- What's your favorite holiday? And what's your second favorite holiday?

5. Fire the negative and positive anchors simultaneously

- When I touch your left knee and your right knee like this, just notice what happens now...
- (important: hold the two triggers for a few moments while the collision happens, and allow for the neurological dust to settle).
- (Important: release the negative anchor a few seconds before you release the positive anchor, to allow the positive energy to fully absorb the remaining negative energy).

6. Test the collapse of the negative anchor

- Most people say that this NLP pattern feels strangely good... perhaps a bit confusing, but in a good way... and that means it's working.
- Now when I fire the negative anchor, has all the energy drained out of it? If no, return to step 5. If yes, proceed to step 7.

7. Reinforce the positive anchor

- Now, I want you to recall that positive state in its full strength. See what you saw here which you heard and feel what you felt you were at the very peak of the positive state.
- And now as you feel this very strongly, I'm going to touch you right here (touch the right knee or the right palm).
- That's right. And now you're going to be able to invoke this resourceful state whenever you need it!

When to Use This Pattern:

Use the Collapsing Anchors pattern when you want to rid yourself or your client of unwanted thoughts or states that seem to arise at just the wrong time.

When this pattern is done effectively, the negative state will just effortlessly melt into the anchored positive state all by itself.

Credits:
John Grinder, and others.

NLP Techniques: Parts Integration

The Idea:

The *Parts Integration* or Parts Negotiation pattern is useful for times when we hold conflicting values, each having a great importance within ourselves. Strong values or desired outcomes are backed by mental and emotional resources, such that when these conflicts happen a real internal struggle can ensue, and one part of ourselves can find itself at war with another. We feel like there is no way out of these dilemmas or conundrums except to let the parts go on fighting.

Occasional dilemmas are a part of life, but when these battles rage on for too long, it can become debilitating. Fortunately whether the conflict is occasional or constant, we can use this NLP pattern to arrive at a win-win or no-deal solution.

The Pattern:

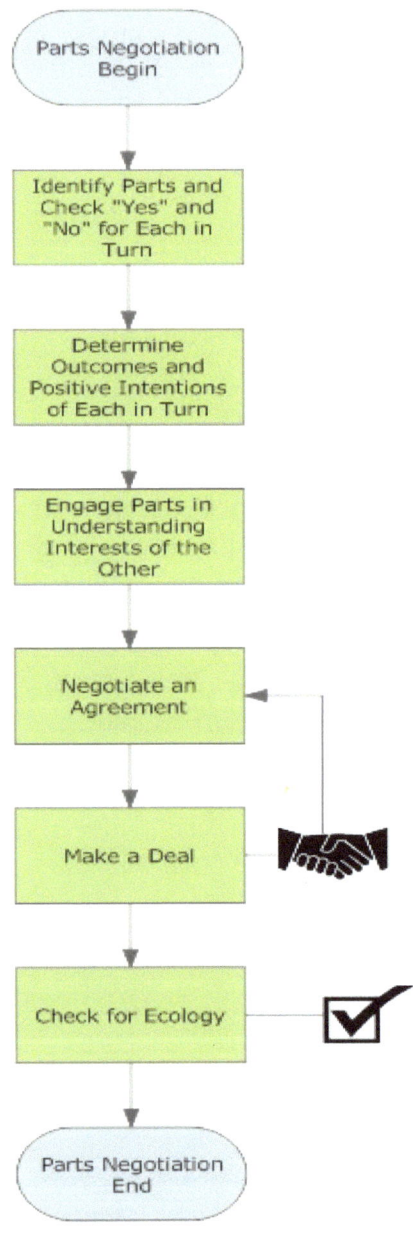

1. Identify the parts, and check for "yes" and "no" for each
• Get in touch with the part of you that does or believes in X... Does it have a name?
• What signal would X like to give us to mean "yes", congruently?
• Now get in touch with the part of you that does or believes in Y... Does it have a name?
• What signal would Y like to give us to mean "yes", congruently?

2. Determine the desired outcomes and positive intentions of each part in turn
• Let's start by giving X an audience... What positive outcome does X want for you... and when X gets that outcome, what does that do for you... and what does that outcome do for you?

- Now, let's give Y a turn... What positive outcome does Y want for you... and when Y gets that outcome, what does that do for you... and what does that outcome do for you?

3. Engage the parts in understanding the interests of the other
- Does X understand and agree with any of the positive intentions of Y? Which, and how much?
- Does Y understand and agree with any of the positive intentions of X? Which, and how much?

4. Negotiate an agreement
- Can X can agree not to interrupt or sabotage Y when it is expressing itself through you?
- Go inside and check for a congruent "yes".
- Can Y can agree to wait its turn to express itself when X holds sway in you?
- Go inside and check for a congruent "yes".

5. Make a deal
- Can both sides agree to cooperate respectfully of each other for the foreseeable future?
- If either side becomes dissatisfied with the other, would it please give a clear sign so that we know it is time to renegotiate? Can that sign be given amicably?

6. Check for *ecology*
- Are there any other parts of you that disagree with this deal?
- Are there any other reasons not to implement this plan now?
- If there are are any incongruencies, return to step 4.

When to Use This Pattern:
This pattern can be used whenever you pick up on

emotionalized speech like "on the one hand..., and on the other hand... I can't decide, and I wind up hating myself!", or "I feel torn by this constant dilemma...!", or "that's the conundrum!" Use this pattern whenever you hear yourself or another using these speech patterns.

Remember that parts are not separate, but just different aspects of our one-self. The goal is always to bring more congruency into more contexts, even when some urges must wait their turn for expression.

Credits:
Richard Bandler, John Grinder, and others.

NLP Techniques: Six-Step Reframing
The Idea:
The Six-Step Reframing Pattern indirectly engages the *unconscious* mind. When there is a shadowy part of you that you just can't put your finger on, but you know is behind some of your inappropriate behaviors, wouldn't it be great if you could just enter into dialogue with that part? If it could just show us a sign, then we could begin to understand it's purpose, and from there negotiate a peace. During this process, we might never know the name or put a face to this unconscious part of us, but that should not stop us from being able to communicate with it. Think of this part as a kind of "dark knight" within you, which though it communicates obliquely via shadows, is really on your side if you can just discover and satisfy its higher intent. This is not unlike Batman, who must ally with Commissioner Gordon and DA Harvey Dent in pursuit of public safety and justice, is it not?
The Pattern:

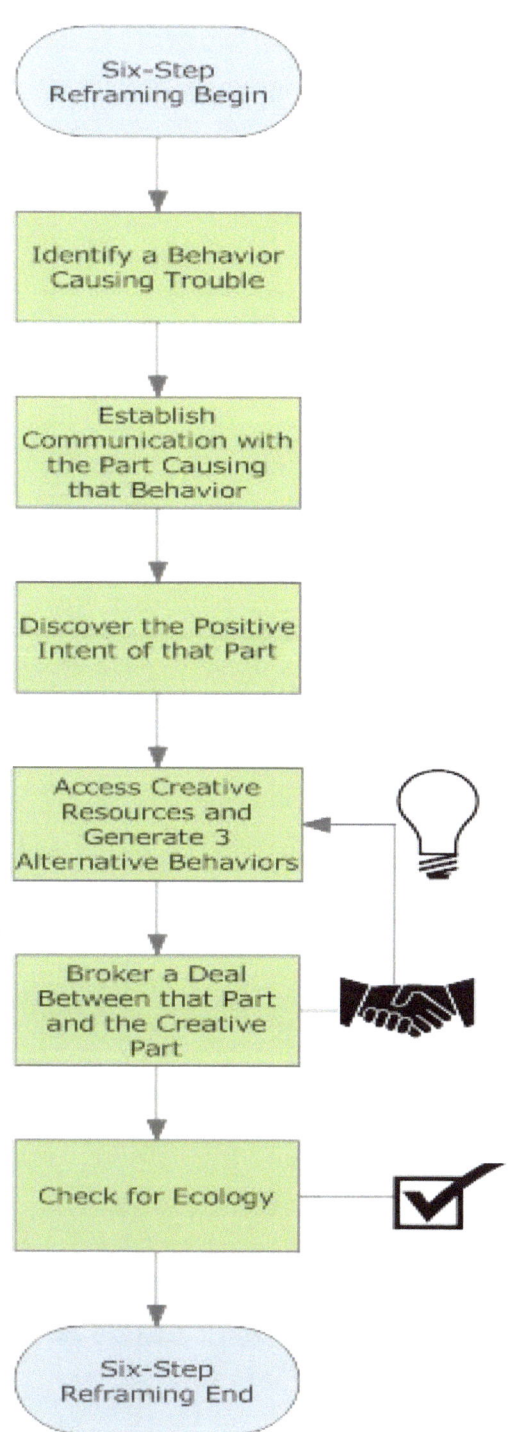

1. Identify a behavior that is causing you trouble

- What behavior do you wish to change, which is subject to inner resistance?
- What compulsive thoughts or actions would you like to change, but can't because there is part of you that won't cooperate?

2. Establish communication with the part that triggers this behavior

- Go inside now and ask for that resistant part of you to reveal itself. Is there a feeling, a sound, a movement, a color or a sensation that let's you know "I'm listening"?
- Ask that part of you if it is willing to communicate with you, and try to discern a yes or no.
- If you get a no, it may be that it does not trust your intent, and so you must assure that part that you will respect its intent, and not abreact, whatever it is.
- If you get a yes, thank the part, and you are ready to proceed.

3. Discover the positive intent of that part

- Ask the part if it is willing to reveal its positive intent to conscious awareness. Trust that the answer will come, and be willing to wait for a yes or a no.
- If you get a yes, then probe the part further to learn if it trusts your conscious judgment.
- Do I allow this positive intent to be expressed?
- Is there a more useful behavior that expresses the same positive intent as well? If you get a no, then you have more trust-work to do here.
- Your part does not trust that solutions you have come up with will work as well.

4. Access creative resources
- Ask your creative center to come up with 3 alternatives to present back to that part. These must be 3 new ideas, different than what you have tried before.
- When you feel that these ideas will really work, then communicate them to this part.

5. Broker a deal and commit the part to the more resourceful behavior
- Will the part that ran the old behavior be willing to run one or more of these new behaviors instead?
- Will the part that ran the old behavior identify the triggers for the new behaviors? What are they?

6. Check for *ecology*
- Is there any part of you that disagrees with running the new behaviors when triggered?
- Are you fully congruent about this?

When to Use This Pattern:
There are parts of us that look out for us, but prefer to remain unnamed. They protect us, but in ways that are suboptimal. Try this whenever you struggle to name the part that manifests this behavior, but you want to seek its cooperation toward a better solution.

The Six-Step Reframing pattern is based on the *metaphor* of an unconscious "part". You must be very comfortable with this metaphor for this pattern to succeed. If you or the client feel awkward or confused about parts, then try something else.

Credits:
Michael Hall, and others.

NLP Techniques: Agreement Frame
The Idea:

The Agreement Frame pattern is useful when two parties cannot agree on something. There are generally 4 strategies one can choose when dealing with disagreement:

- Get Out
- Give In
- Take Over
- Go for the Win-Win

There are certainly times when getting out, giving in, or taking over is the appropriate response, usually determined by whether the one's safety, or relationship or the *outcome* is the primary concern, and the other concerns are subordinated.

Going for win-win is the *context* where this NLP pattern is most effective, because the effort to walk through the pattern takes time and effort up front. When both parties decide the outcome and the relationship are both worth preserving, then it is worth their investment of time, effort and emotion. When it is established that both parties must have a stake in a favorable outcome, then it is time to begin. Now let's revisit why disagreements happen in the first place... People operate from their frames, consisting of values, priorities or categories of things in the world. When these frames are misaligned and the two parties are too inflexible to see the matter through the frames of the other, then it is time to go meta... or rather assume a higher frame that encompasses the frames of the two parties.

The Pattern:

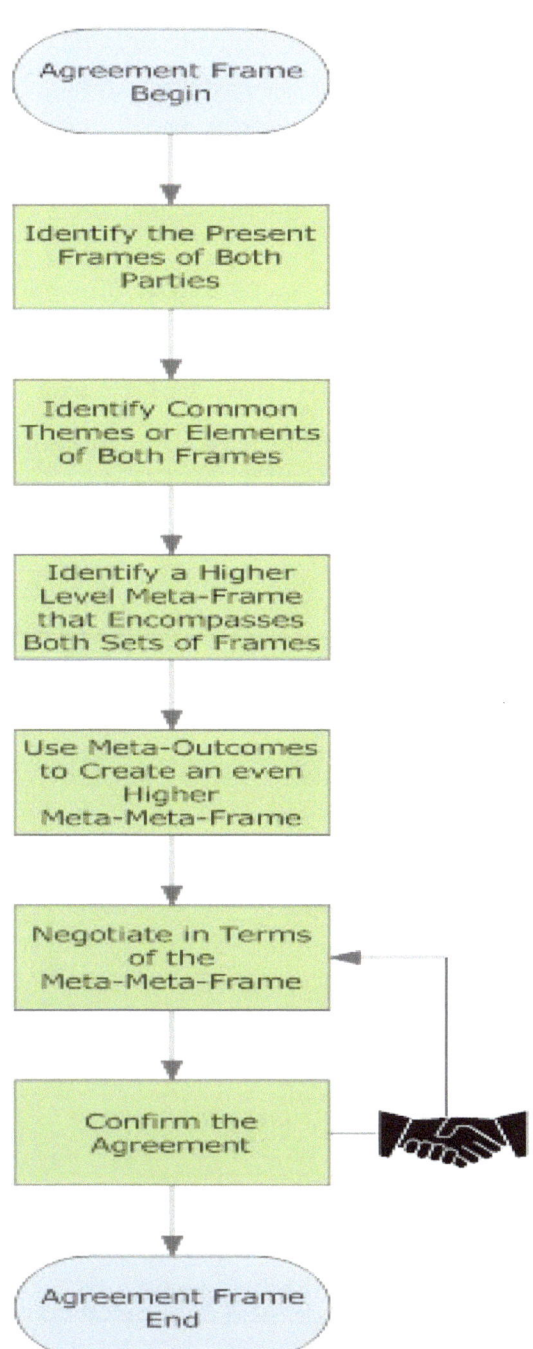

As you walk through this pattern, it really helps to write down the answers you will get, so they are not lost sight of during the process.

1. Identify the present frames of both parties
- Ask each party in turn: What specifically do you want?
- Ask each party in turn: What is important to you about that outcome? 1 - 10?

2. Identify common themes or elements of both frames
- Is there a common ultimate outcome for both parties?

3. Identify a higher-level meta-frame that encompasses both sets of frames
- Ask each party in turn: If you get what you want, what will that do or get for you? What does it buy you?

4. Use meta-level outcomes of both parties to create an even higher meta-frame
- Ask each party in turn: And when you get that higher outcome or purpose, then what does that get for you?

5. Frame the negotiation in terms of the meta-meta-frame

By now, if there is no common ground... DO NOT PROCEED! Check again to reconfirm that both parties want to resolve the issue, and establish common ground, then backtrack as necessary until a common frame is established. If it is clear to everyone where the common ground is, then proceed.
- Ask each party to contribute solutions to making sure both sides meet the terms of the higher frame generally, while getting both parties specifically what they want as much as

possible.
- If specifics must be traded off, then what can those specifics be while preserving the relationship and meeting the terms of higher frame?

6. Confirm the agreements
- Once agreements are reached and written down, confirm the understanding of the terms of the agreement with both parties mutually. Clarify, backtrack and revise as required.

When to Use this Pattern:
Use the Agreement Frame pattern when the relationship and the outcomes are both too important to sacrifice either one. This works in business, marriages, and between friends. Sometimes the process takes only a few minutes or hours... or it can go on for days or weeks whenever the stakes and complexity are high. Very complex issues require professional and often legal counsel.

Credits:
Michael Hall, Stephen Covey, Dudley Lynch and others

NLP Techniques: Aligning Neurological Levels
The Idea:
Aligning *Neurological Levels*, or the Aligned Self Pattern is one of my very favorite NLP patterns, because it can be a whole intervention in itself. It is based on the work of Robert Dilts, who discovered that people operate at different levels at different times, and when these levels are out of alignment with each other, people not only feel stuck, they are perceptibly stuck.

Like the Circle of Excellence, this pattern works

extremely well both with individuals and in groups. This pattern is good for both remedial and generative work.
The Pattern:

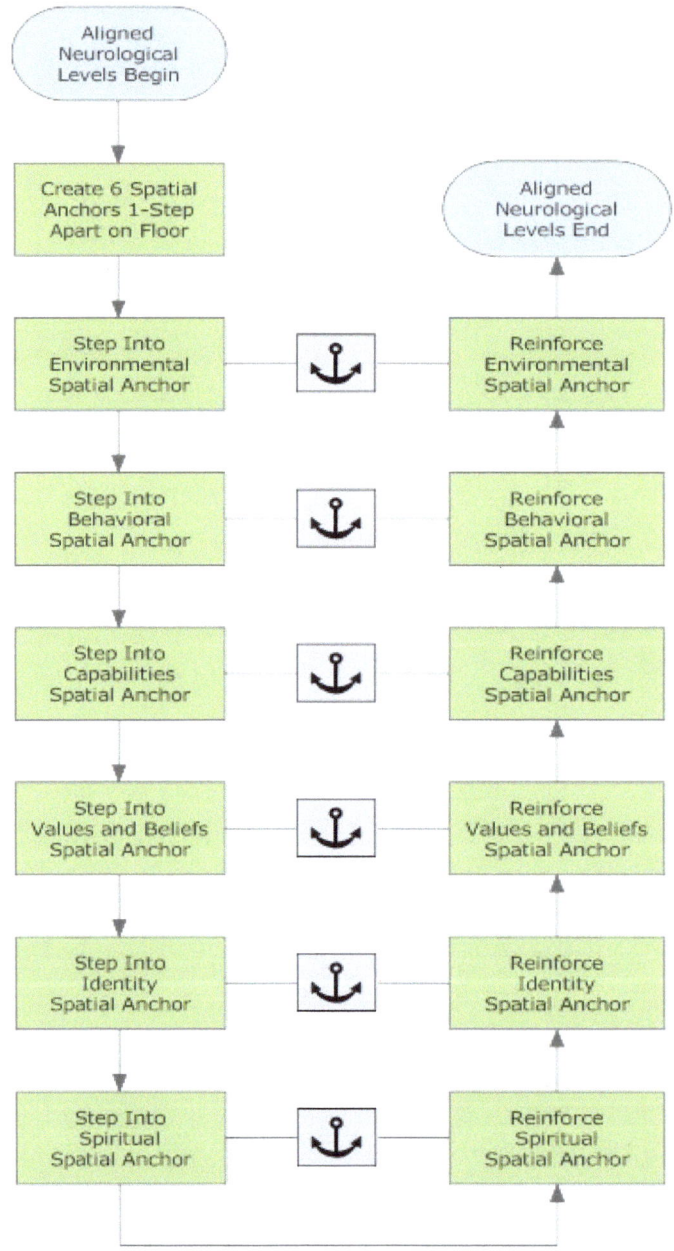

1. Create 6 Spatial Anchors 1-Step Apart on the Floor

Lay down 6 cards or coins about 1 step apart on the floor extending out in front of the explorer.
Each one of the cards will be spatially anchored as follows:
- *Environment* (i.e. times and places)
- Behaviors (i.e. behaviors, thoughts and states)
- Capabilities (i.e. resources and skills)
- Values and Beliefs (i.e. what's important or necessary)
- *Identity* (i.e. who and what you are)
- Spirit (i.e. highest intent and purpose, who else is touched)

2. Step Into the Environmental Spatial Anchor
- Think of the times and places where you will want and need to be as congruent and resourceful as possible.
- Think of another time and place where you will want and need these resources.

3. Step Into the Behavioral Spatial Anchor
- Now, take a step forward into the next space, and think of all the behaviors you will need to achieve your *outcome*... your state, your thoughts and attitude, your posture and breathing, the way you speak and move.

4. Step Into the Capabilities Spatial Anchor
- Now, take a step forward into the next space, and think of all the resources, skills, knowledge, people, information, strengths and abilities you will need to achieve your outcome...
- Make sure these resources are ecologically sound... good.

5. Step Into the Values and Beliefs Spatial Anchor

- Now, take a step forward and imagine the kinds of beliefs and values that serve you in achieving your outcome.
- Take a moment to state those positive beliefs to yourself and notice how they support you in achieving your outcome.
- Take a moment to organize your values so that first things come first... good.

6. Step Into the Identity Spatial Anchor

- Now, take a step forward to notice how well who you are aligns with your pursuit and achievement of your outcome.
- Take a moment to more perfectly align your identity with this pursuit... good... that's it.

7. Step Into the *Spiritual* Spatial Anchor

- Now, take a final step into the realm of the eternal. Reflect on the positive legacy your contributions have left for mankind and posterity.
- Take a moment to experience how that will look, sound and feel to have done something positive for others, and allow that experience to soak in, now.

8. Reinforce the Spiritual Spatial Anchor

- Now, turn around 180 degrees and face the direction you came.
- Take a moment now to reflect on how this highest purpose and intent can inform, modulate and enlighten all other aspects of your life.

9. Reinforce the Identity Spatial Anchor

- Now take a step forward, and having experienced the eternal perspective, notice now how your identity has been deeply shaped in powerful ways.

- Take a moment to project how this more powerful you will engage in the world.

10. Reinforce the Values and Beliefs Spatial Anchor
- Now take a step forward, and having updated what it means to be you now, notice how your beliefs and values are informed, revised, updated and aligned naturally and easily.
- Notice how easily it is to recognize and place first things first. Now imagine how those important things will easily get done, and how the less important things can also get done in due time.
- Notice how confident you feel that you are also doing the right things.

11. Reinforce the Capabilities Spatial Anchor
- Now take a step forward, and having updated and revised your priorities, values and beliefs, notice how your learning is accelerated, focused on what you'll need when you'll need it.
- Notice also how your confidence and competence have also grown up side-by-side and how they support each other. Notice yourself in a flow state, enjoying being good at what you do now.

12. Reinforce the Behavioral Spatial Anchor
- Now take a step forward, and see yourself as a detached observer, performing with confidence and competence those new skills and capabilities, and notice how your thoughts, emotions, posture, breathing, expression, speech, motions, decisions are all enhanced and perfected.
- And now just step into that experience as

yourself and see, hear and feel yourself doing these things as naturally, smoothly and easily as you saw your self when detached... good.

13. Reinforce the Environmental Spatial Anchor
Finally, take a last step forward, and bring all of these new resources, skills, powers into real-projected future places and times. See yourself doing everything fully congruent in these situations, notice what day and time it is, what you are wearing, who is present, and just feel great!

When to Use this Pattern:
Align Neurological Levels as a great group introduction to NLP. This is also an excellent exercise to finish off a chain of NLP interventions, because it reinforces and integrates learnings covering the gamut across all levels of experience. Do try this exercise, it comes highly recommended. NLP Comprehensive also favors this exercise during their integration week at the end of Practitioner training, and for good reason!

Credits: Robert Dilts

Self Identity NLP Patterns
NLP Techniques: Who am I?

Of all aspects of life that Neuro-Linguistic Programming can assist with, helping to define and enhance our self-concept is among the most powerful. I personally love working with *identity*, because self expression is one of the strongest urges our experience. A change in identity has profound changes in all other areas and activities of life.

The clearer we become about who we are as individuals, the more naturally we stand out and simultaneously integrate with others in the world. In life, we can evolve through stages of dependence, through independence, and then achieve inter-dependence as Stephen Covey says. Mihaly Csikszentmihalyi says growth and one's identity (self) is supported by a purposeful life filled with flowful experiences. Flow creates increasingly complex people that are at once more individuated and more integrated. Joseph Campbell's work tells that human life can be a journey wherein the hero of the story (one's self) progresses from a naive dependent individual through a series of adventures which define him or her. The hero then becomes a master of two worlds: the inner world, and the outer world being shaped by the inner and outer worlds, and shaping it in turn. Socrates urged us all to "know thyself". This is the ideal life.

Yeah, but who am I?

When is the last time you have asked yourself a question like one of these:
- Do I have any worth?
- How important am I?
- What talents, skills or abilities can I call my own?
- Am I a lovable or attractive person?
- Who do others say that I am?
- Do I deserve to enjoy life?

Our identity is a fragile thing. It is constantly under threat of entropy and disintegration. One sure thing is that who we are is always changing. We are not the same person we were a day or a month or a year ago. We've changed in subtle or obvious ways. Sometimes who we are changes for the better, and sometimes for the worse. Thousands of

books, movies and songs turn on this truth.
We often get stuck, or all twisted up, or sideways as our self concepts develop in less than optimal ways. Often we grow up to become what others want or expect us to be, wearing a mask as it were, and creating inner resistance. Other times, our concept of self is tamped down by critical voices coming from outside or inside ourselves. Abuse during childhood is a direct attack on the child's own self concept, which NLP techniques can help to redefine. At other times, we are simply not aware of our own possibilities, and NLP patterns can help here too.

How Can NLP Help?

This section presents proven NLP Techniques and Patterns that can help the individual define him or herself in new ways, strengthen and tune up one's already healthy self concept, or re-imprint a stunted childhood self-concept with a more empowered and resourceful one. Once we know who we are, why we are here, and have resources at our disposal to fully express ourselves, the details just seem to work themselves out, do they not? Let's get started...

NLP Techniques: Disidentification
The Idea:

Many times circumstances and emotions rule our lives precisely because we think that we are our circumstances and emotions. Outside of NLP, disidentification is a central theme to many *spiritual* and self-help movements. Eckhart Tolle points to identification with our problems as the source of all human suffering, and he may be right.

We are not our circumstances, nor are we our

emotions. We are more than that. We are not our bodies, we are more than that too. The gist of this pattern is to reframe one's thinking, so that we come to know experientially that we have a body, but we are not our body. We have circumstances, but we are not those circumstances. We have problems, but we are not our problems. We have emotions, but we are not our emotions. We have thoughts and experiences, but we are not those thoughts or experiences. At the core, we are the consciousness having all of these things, and while these things can change, our core remains safely untouched.

Separating our core *identity* from these aspects of experience is powerful. It is the beginning of wisdom and the start of a new life for someone who is completely identified with his or her illness, relationship, job, wealth, or story. It is also very scary when identification with these things is very strong. It can feel like part of their identity is being severed at first, and then the realization comes that what was severed was not their identity at all, but only a figment… a hallucination. This being said, realize that this pattern will be met with resistance by most Westerners, and Americans in particular. The Western mentality holds a deep fear of separating one's identity from one's thoughts and feelings. At worst, it seems like a kind of death, and at the very least a challenge to separate one's identity from their thoughts, feelings, beliefs and story will make no sense at first.

The Pattern:

1. Test willingness to accept higher core identity

- Do you accept the notion that you are more than your circumstances, health, wealth and relationships?
- Do you accept the notion that you are more than your thoughts and feelings?
- Do you accept the notion that you are more than your roles and duties?
- Do you accept the notion that you are more than your body?
- Are you willing to explore these ideas further to get in touch with that higher self?

Note: If they are not willing to go further, stop here. You may ask them to say more about their unwillingness, but do not continue with this pattern until they are ready to play.

2. Use linguistic patterns to start to dis-identify

- How does it feel to you to say "I have a body, but I am not my body"?
- How does it feel to you to say "I have a job, but I am not my job"?
- How does it feel to you to say "I have money, but I am not my money"?
- How does it feel to you to say "I have a religion, but I am not my religion"?
- How does it feel to you to say "I have a _____, but I am not my _____"?
- How could you express this in a way that seems better or more true to you?

3. Induce relaxation to strengthen the dis-identification

- As you relax into a comfortable and safe *state* of mind… invite a higher self capable of thinking transcendentally about who you are to become activated.
- Allow that higher self to step back, and safely and

objectively evaluate the differences between your essential core, and other aspects of yourself that are separate from that essential core.

4. While in *trance*, separate self from circumstances and functions

- As you fully come to realize those aspects of your former self as being only an extension, a function or a tool of your core self... notice how safe and valuable your core self can remain with or without them.
- Notice how those extensions are not the same as who you are at the core.
- Notice how from the higher self you can call upon those extensions, functions or tools as required.

5. Ask the brain to create a higher self

- Have you gotten in touch with the you that is above and beyond your things, your thoughts, emotions and feelings? Some people call this the watcher, the listener, the observer or the master of what goes on in the body-mind.
- Ask your brain to create a space for that higher self to be. Have you got it? Good.

6. Strengthen the higher self as a permanent and ongoing entity

- Would you be willing to allow your higher self to freely observe your thoughts, feelings and attachments into the future?
- As you contemplate this new kind of mindfulness into the future, are there any parts of it that make you uncomfortable?
- Take some time to be with the higher mind as you go into the future. Let that integrate into

your work life, home life, relationships, etc.

When to Use This Pattern:
Use this pattern with yourself, a loved one or a client whose emotional overreactions to stress, loss or feelings of doom are overwhelming. They may feel like they are dying in the face of changing circumstances, health, wealth or relationships. Using this pattern can help them to explore and come to know for themselves that bad things can happen to them, but their core self will remain safe and secure. This pattern is particularly useful in cases where fanatic *behavior* is driven by identification with some cause.

Warning: Only do this pattern with their consent! It is not OK to delve into matters of identity against their will. If you try to do so, you will be met with overt or covert resistance, as the ego is fighting for its very existence.

Credits:
Michael Hall, and others.

NLP Applications
What are the Applications of NLP?
Some people are mainly interested NLP applications, or what NLP can do, and how and when it can be used. In other words, what are the jobs for the tool? Some of the NLP applications are quite ubiquitous like phobia cures, allergy cures, *modeling*, coaching and persuasion, while others are very much less charted. This online book is dedicated to exploring NLP applications.

I like to think of NLP as a toolset to help us move from where we are to where we want to be, which is a very portable definition across many, many contexts. Essentially, you can fill in the blanks in

any way you like, to begin to understand how many unique circumstances NLP can be applied to :
- I want to experience more or less _____.
    (e.g. joy, worthy, grief, relaxation, anger)
- I want to stop _____. (e.g. smoking, pornography, blowing up, drinking, nightmares)
- I want to feel _____. (e.g. better, happier, thinner, more confident)
- I want to have more or less _____. (e.g. time, love, joy, money, debt)
- I want to be more or less _____. (e.g. productive, funny, shy, attractive, healthy)

Of course you could add your own examples to the list, but you get the idea. As long as you are using your mind to improve on your situation, you could say you are using NLP in one form or another, whether or not you are doing so consciously, or whether or not what you are doing has a name associated with it.

NLP Distills What Works into Repeatable Patterns

NLP observes behaviors that work in a variety of contexts. and those habits or strategies that get us what we want or need, will have some habits, patterns, commonalities, regularities or structures that can be studied, learned and taught. After the pattern is boiled down, we find that the simpler the pattern, the easier it is to master, repeat, teach, and modify to suit a particular circumstance.

Some NLPer's compare these structures to jazz, which has a structure (*unconscious* to those who are not jazz musicians, conscious to those who are), and that structure allows those musicians to jam around that structure in syncopated harmony and melody.

Some of the most common NLP patterns are explained in detail here.

NLP Patterns Only Work When Applied to Context and Universal Needs

It would be a mistake to suppose that we can do NLP in a vacuum. As living beings, we are part of many interdependent spheres of influence, including biological spheres, cultural spheres, social spheres, mental spheres, *spiritual* spheres, etc. So NLP applications must satisfy the needs of real people in the real world, and the subjective maps that chart that world. Everybody has needs for safety, acceptance, self-expression and meaning. If these needs are ignored, the NLP intervention will simply not work.

NLP patterns can work wonderfully in one context, and can also be impotent in other contexts. Likewise the same pattern in similar contexts can only be effective across many individuals only if it is informed by where those individuals want to go, and where they are coming from.

NLP Application = NLP Techniques => Appropriate Context

When NLP patterns are applied to an appropriate context we have an NLP application. The tool is mated to the job, and the result is change work at the neurological level.

For example, addiction recovery is a powerful application of swish patterns or compulsion blowout patterns in a therapeutic context. Seduction would be an application of persuasive language patterns in a dating context. Family counseling would be an application of positive intent, and re-imprinting. Wealth creation might be an application of *timeline* or *parts integration* patterns in a coaching context.

NLP Healthy Body Mind
No Longer the Picture of Health
While industrialized nations have conquered many infectious diseases of a century ago, and are living longer than ever on average, we are increasingly falling prey to new diseases of our own making. Industrialized nations are among the sickest on earth due to our *environment* and lifestyles. Stress, carcinogens, toxins, obesity and sleep deprivation all combine to erode the quality of life and lead to higher rates of diabetes, cancer, depression, suicide. Our biology is just not able to keep pace and evolve fast enough to cope with the changes that profit-seeking industrialization and technology have produced.

Healthy Mind in a Healthy Body
The ancient Greeks got many things right, including the maxim "Healthy Mind in a Healthy Body". Notice the neither they nor I said a scholarly mind in an an perfectly athletic body. That is not the point here. The point is that for the mind or the body to function optimally in service of a healthy and productive life, they should both be healthy. Neurolinguistic Programming (NLP) understands that the mind and body are two facets of the whole person, and that any intervention must take the wholeness of both into account. The mind and the body have profound influences on each other, and are chemically and neurologically inseparable. A sick mind will pull the body down eventually, just as a sick body will pull the mind down a notch or two.

Conversely, exercise makes one feel better, reason better, and remember more, just as a mind that is not preoccupied by anxiety eats less, sleeps better, and has more energy to direct in useful directions.

Taking care of the whole person from youth through old age is paramount in one's happiness. Living forever is unrealistic, but living as well as we can for as long as we can is not.

How Neurolinguistic Programming Can Improve Health

Modeling Success

Remember that the heart of NLP has always been modeling excellence, and with regards to health it is no different. Find out what works, who's doing it, and copy them. Not for the short run (there are no shortcuts in good health), but for the long run. This includes modeling what works for people who have always been healthy, as well as those that once were not, but now are and have maintained it for a while. The lives of healthy people are often different at many different levels from those of less healthy people, and through NLP those levels can be modeled, including:

- **Spirituality** (what is the higher purpose and intent of healthy people?)
- *Identity* (who do healthy people believe they are, and what principles of health do they identify with?)
- **Beliefs and Values** (what do healthy people believe about their minds and bodies, and why is it important to put their health high on their lists?)
- **Capabilities** (what are healthy people able to do to make time for health, and what does their

health enable them to do in life?)
- **Behaviors** (what do healthy people do for meals, exercise, activity, recreation, stress relief, rest? what are their do's and don'ts?)
- **Environment** (what and who do healthy people surround themselves with, and what do they not permit into their homes or work places?)

Compare what you find by asking these questions to models of health, and compare with your own? If you see any differences, these can serve as places to start.

Developing *Rapport* with One's Body

Another key principle of Neurolinguistic Programming is rapport. Traditionally, rapport has meant to convey like-mindedness to another person, but in the *context* of health, it is vitally important to be in touch and in rapport with one's own body. We need to understand non-verbal chemical signals to indicate fatigue, true hunger, satiety or fullness, pain and pleasure. Most people live in their heads, and regard their bodies as transportation for their heads only. Once you pay attention to your body and learn its language, you will eat right, sleep right, exercise right, and the whole process need not drive you crazy because you get your head out of the loop.

Education is also required, because there are psychological and chemical assaults on your mind and body specifically engineered to send your body and mind false and confusing signals. Every smoker knows that smoking calms the nerves and brings a temporary sense of relaxation and control, while abstinence produces a tremendous case of nerves, yet we know cognitively that smoking is a slow but sure death. Every carb addict knows that you can't eat just one potato chip. The refined carbs, salts, synthetic fats and preservatives assault the pleasure centers of the brain and switch off the ability to easily say enough, at the same time the body is thrashing out metabolic hormones to try to deal with the unnatural substances you've just absorbed into your blood. NLP can help you learn to pay attention to your body throughout the day, and over a lifetime, verbalize what is happening at a chemical level, and respond with what your body needs, naturally rather than synthetically.

Love the Body and Mind You've Got
You can't be someone else, but you can be a better you! Your health can be measured in terms of how good *you* feel and look, and how good *your* numbers are. If you go from 20 lbs overweight to 10 lbs overweight in 6 months, take yourself to a movie! If your HDL rises by 20 points and your LDL lowers 15 points since your last checkup, buy yourself a new pair of shoes! If you could do 6 pushups 6 months ago and can now do 60, then flaunt it! Small, incremental improvements over time do count, and make all the difference in your mood, energy, and ability to enjoy and contribute to life.

NLP Relationships
Neurolinguistic Programming Fosters Multiple Perspectives
Neurolinguistic Programming (NLP) is famous for helping people gain new perspectives on problematic areas. What better area than in relationships to gain multiple perspectives? As the saying goes, it takes two to tango, so in addition to

seeing our own perspective, it is imperative to also develop the ability to see the world through the eyes and feelings of our partner.

NLP offers other key learning on relationships, such as the notion that the word "relationship" is itself a *nominalization*. NLP says that all nominalizations are intangible nouns which mask a deeper set of meanings and processes, which are unique to every person you ask. Perhaps the biggest shock for newlyweds is to discover that a "marriage" does not exist at all... there is his marriage, and her marriage, and those two mind-held notions are quite different to say the least. A nominalization such as relationship even means different things to the same person and different times and in different contexts.

There is No Such Think as a Relationship in NLP

Keep in mind that Neurolinguistic Programming regards relating as a process, not a thing... which is so powerful because a process can be changed, whereas a thing often cannot. In NLP, relating is a verb, not a noun. Relating has a structure, made up of *identity*, beliefs, values, skills, behaviors, and it happens in some *environment*. NLP would not ask "what is it about your relationship that you don't like", rather it would ask "what is it about your relating that is not working". This line of questioning allows room to maneuver and change what is not working. You can't change a relationship... it does not exist! You can change the way you are relating, and that is powerful!

NLP in Dating
No Quick NLP Seduction Techniques Here!
Sorry, dear reader. To save us both time. anyone looking for NLP tricks to rapidly and rapidly and covertly seduce their dating partners can move on to other more qualified authors. Respectfully, you won't find that information here. But if you're interested the long view, sprinkled with a little *ecology*, adventure and bliss, then you are in the right place.

Neurolinguistic Programming Models Success
Remember that at the Heart of NLP is the *modeling* of successful strategies in others, so that we can make those strategies our own. Those people we model may be famous, but not necessarily so. When dating for the long run, think of other couples that have stood the test of time and got happier the longer they were together, and ask them how they did it. You may get some other strategies, but I'll share a couple here.

Dating *Strategy* No. 1: It's Easier to Pick 'em than to Train 'em
This first strategy is really a *belief*, but whether you believe it or not, it is a useful posture when approaching dating. Is it not true that we only marry who we date? Except for my Eastern friends who's parents and inlaws did all the vetting up front, the rest of us tend to shack up with someone we get to know from our own dating pool of one or more. (If you find this is not true for you, I'd love to hear about it).

Whether dating broadly, or narrowing the field we tend to date partners that are a reflection of who we *think* we are or *imagine* that we want to be. More than anything else, we humans need an

identity in the world, and we will fight and die to preserve it. Virginia Satir pointed out that this urge is stronger than the urge to live. So people don't date each other... egos date each other.
After selecting a partner, we tend to continue together when who we *think* we are is directly or indirectly reinforced by the other person. Otherwise, we tend to split or continue suffering together when we learn that the other will never conform to our self-constructed identity. To continue in relationship with such a person is the very definition of hell (or at least one definition).
So why would anyone want go as far as marriage without ever probing "who am I, and what do I want?", and "who are you, and what do you want?", and finally "how can we help each other get what we want most?"
The reasons for rushing past the important questions are as nutty as they come, aren't they? Here are a few good one's I've heard:
- He/she was rich (or at least I thought so)...
- I thought I could change him/her...
- My parents though he/she was wonderful...
- He/she turned me on...
- We went to the same church...
- It was foreordained...
- I was drunk...
- I never dated anyone else...
- We both liked dogs...
- We were great in bed...
- It was time...
- I couldn't stand to be alone...
- He/she reminded me of someone else...
- I couldn't say no...

... and I'm sure you have some zingers of your

own. This stuff is the fodder of both stand-up and sit-down comedy, and we laugh because we are all guilty of rushing in to some degree. That's why the jokes are so damned funny, and we all know that to laugh is better than to cry.

Dating Strategy No. 2: My Story is Dating Your Story

Would you pay to see a movie that was was a careful splicing together of "Moulin Rouge" and "Die Hard". Me neither. Know your story, and don't mind telling it, but remember it's your story, and then remember that your date has their own story too. As you're getting to know your date better, the strategy is to try thinking about it that way. What is the plot? What is the theme? Who are the actors? Who gets it in the end? Taking a step back and evaluating your date in terms of their story is both entertaining and insightful.

Anyone can sit through a bad for a couple of hours, and then you're only out a few bucks. If your date's story is really good, and matches your own in important ways, you and your date know there is going to be a sequel.

Dating Strategy No. 3: Take it Slow, and Think with Both Brains

Why would we put more effort into picking a car, or a horse, or a stock than a partner? Figuratively speaking, every dater has two brains, and not enough blood to work them both at the same time. Now, eventually the blood does find its way to the other brain, but we require a few alternating cycles to come to a fuller understanding between them both. Attraction waxes and wanes, and when it wanes, support for the whole person must be there too.

Dating Strategy No. 4: Find a New Meaning for "No"

So here is some advice you won't get anywhere else... To get a full yes, you need to go through a lot of no's. *Go for the no!* The problem with this advice is that most daters associate fear, regret, embarrassment or shame with a no, so they'll do anything to avoid it. *Daters: you're afraid of the wrong thing. A no can sting a little, but a superficial yes can kill you.*

The best think NLP can do for a dater is to associate better meaning and feelings with a no, so that the dater can be honest, expressive about what they want, and through the dating process eventually arrive at a full yes.

NLP in Marriage
Aah, marriage...

...Complete with a wedding, the honeymoon, and then...

Everything they ever told me about marriage at home, in my religion, in the locker room, my family science class, and every sitcom I ever watched was to say the least, quite far afield from the actual subjective experience of my own marriage once it materialized. Every one of my pre-conceptions of marriage involved a dissociated image of myself with my future wife and kids, which was associated only by warm and fuzzy feelings. Marriage is dissociated imagined experience right up until you're in one, then you finally discover all the realities that come from being associated *in* the experience! As long as marriage was dissociated and in my future, I *knew* that I would not make the same mistakes as everyone else in the world.

Once I was associated into a marriage of my own, I experienced the ecstacy, frustration, clarity and confusion of marriage for myself. All the jokes about marriage suddenly took on a more visceral aspect.

A second major realization about marriage was that my own subjective experience of marriage was completely different than that of my wife. In essence, we didn't share a common marriage, there was her version, and his (for those readers of same-gender marriage, I'm sure you can make the leap in my meaning to your own situation here).

I laugh and cry at and with people who confess to spending more time doing homework when buying a car than in finding a mate. It's funny, seriously! When I ask why didn't you do more homework before going into a life-long contract with your spouse, the usual answer is *they didn't know how*. So this article is about the how or the structure behind what works before and after the wedding.

So how can NLP help *leading* up to, and after the wedding? How can NLP help marriages to not only survive, but thrive? Let's exercise several basic NLP premises:

- *Nominalization* is Really Process!
- States Change!
- Know What You Want!
- Check *Ecology*!
- Sharpen Your *Sensory Acuity*!
- The Meaning of Communication is the Response You Get!
- If Something is Not Working, Try Something Else!
- Bonus Advice (keep reading to find out)

Let's take these one-at-a-time, shall we?

Nominalization is Really Process

To set the frame for the rest of the ideas to follow know that marriages are a process, and not a thing. Marriages do not exist in the real world. Marriages are a an ongoing concern, a living expression of two people sharing (or not) their dreams, agendas, goals, frustrations, feelings, conversations, silences, attitudes, mistakes, offenses, defenses, quirks, joy, anxiety, pain, etc., etc. Each of these expressions are processes and strategies in themselves, and no expression is exactly alike across couples, or even across time for the same couple.

The main point here is that the person you married is really a stranger to some degree, no matter how well you thought you knew them. Replacing preconceptions with curiousity as you continue to get to know your fiance or spouse goes much further and deeper than becoming complacently assuming about them.

States Change

The state you were in before breakfast is not the same as the state you were in after a big lunch. Energy, attention, interests, moods and priorities shift around dozens of times each day, not to mention in the span of weeks, months or years. Feelings of love wax and want, and our partners become more or less attractive depending on their state and our own. Really observe this in yourself and your partner, and accept it as you would accept the tide.

The better you get to know all your states and those of your partner, the better equipped you are to pace and lead yourself and your partner to a better state, or get out of the way when necessary. Part of knowing your states is also to notice the triggers that evoke states in yourself and your partner. This way, you can use your NLP skills to change behaviors and the *environment* to support more resourceful states. With skill, you can learn to lengthen the peaks and shorten the valleys.

Know What You Both Want

Until you know what you *value* in life and in a partner, feel free to date but do not get married. Otherwise, alignment of *identity*, beliefs and values happens purely by accident. Too many people go their whole lives living a miserable marriage because they did not take the time or did not know how to get in touch with and really vivify their identities, beliefs and values.

NLP always starts with a *well-formed outcome*, then achieving that outcome is just a matter of time and energy.

Check Ecology

Ecology goes far beyond taking your fiance to meet your parents, two intelligent beings are forming a merger, and to he (or she) who sees the future most clearly will go the spoils. Some NLP questions come to mind in better seeing all aspects of the future: 1) what will happen if we do this? 2) what will happen if we don't do this? 3) what won't happen if we do this? 4) what won't happen if we don't do this?

Ask these questions to yourself and your partner, and together you'll better know if you go forward, or just remain friends.

Sharpen Your Sensory Acuity

Nothing is more indicative in the long-term happiness of a marriage quite like the quality of attending to the needs of the other, moment to moment, day to day, and year to year. When the quality of attending to the other suffers, then so does the marriage. Note that attending is a very special verb, and process. You know it when you see it in action.

To attend to your needs and your partner's, you first need to *notice* those needs. Neurolinguistic Programming stresses ongoing development of sensory acuity such that consciously noticing at the beginning eventually becomes unconsciously appropriate responses. This includes attending to responses in physiology, states, surroundings all to make yourself and your partner more comfortable together. There is more communication going on than what is verbalized, and to the really attentive the noise is reduced while the signals are strengthened.

The Meaning of Communication is the Response You Get

This NLP presupposition is a really good shared mantra for all couples. Given that our states fluctuate constantly and that we constantly move in and out of our personal trances, and owing to different backgrounds and communication styles, what we mean to say is never guaranteed to be taken the way we intended it to be.

Couples who allow the freedom to ask what the other person meant to say or convey not only avoid pain and lost time, but gain a richer understanding of the other person's *map of reality*. Asking for clarity is the ideal, but more often than not it needs to be cultivated. Acknowledge and thank your partner any time he or she asks for more clarity, and giving you the chance to update what you said, or even update your own meaning of what was said.

If Something is Not Working, Try Something Else

The way we relate to our parents, to our bosses, to children, neighbors and strrangers does not always work with a spouse. Keep this in mind as you individualize your approach to your spouse.

I knew a couple who regarded their marriage as a laboratory. They were constantly trying out new ideas for relating in fresh ways. Sometimes they consulted books and friends for new ideas, but their real secret weapon was just observing what made the other person smile, and sometimes they just asked the other. Novel idea!

If you need to talk, and the other person needs space right now, try inviting the other person to take the time they need, and let you know when they are ready for the talk. Honor the needs of both, and eventually the time will come to be heard... fully.

Never Do NLP *ON* Your Partner, Do NLP *WITH* Your Partner

It goes without saying that if you or your spouse use NLP to manipulate or coerce the other into doing something they don't want or agree to do willingly, you are inflicting real damage on your intimacy and trust. Don't say I didn't warn you!

NLP Wealth Mindset
Can Neurolinguistic Programming Create Wealth?

Neurolinguistic Programming models excellence in special humans in terms of mental strategies, and then teach that excellence to other humans (typically those who can afford the book, the training, or who funded the *modeling* studies within their own organizations). So how do we model wealth creation and maintenance, and teach that for free? Well, first we must ask "who's gonna do that for free?", and then listen to the sucking sound as nobody replies. I'll address that here.

Before NLP, Napolean Hill modeled the magnates of *Think and Grow Rich* fame, and millions of copies were sold in dozens of languages. Certainly now there are many more millionaires walking the earth than in those days (partly due to inflation, partly due to technology and a stable economy, and partly due to people learning how to become millionaires through the example of others like those modeled in *Think and Grow Rich*). But why is not every reader of the book a millionaire? How do we apply the lessons of *Think and Grow Rich* to every man? Can NLP help?

Certainly. It's not that the lessons of *Think and Grow Rich* are not true. They are. It's that *Think and Grow Rich* is based on general principles. Virginia Satir taught that nothing happens in general... everything happens in the specific. We have to start wealth building where we are, with what we've got, and this book will address how NLP can help to do just that.

NLP Training: What is Consciousness?

Like me, you may have friends and connections on a mission to "raise consciousness", as though this would be the solution to the world's problems. Other friends of mine never give consciousness a thought, or simply just dismiss the topic of consciousness as something new age people talk about a lot.

I'm always curious to know how people define

consciousness, and what they mean by raising it. Do they mean adding more consciousness to the consciousness we already have? Do they mean moving our consciousness somehow from a lower to a higher level? And if so, then who defines the levels? Are these levels of behavioral strategies? Are they levels of values and beliefs? Are they levels of esoteric experience? What are other words for consciousness? Mindfulness? Awareness? Waking time? Paying attention? Which of these aspects are trying to be raised, and who says that our consciousness needs to be raised anyway? Why? In whose service? So many questions about such a vaguely wonderful term. Within the consciousness community, I can't seem to find two people able to agree on what consciousness is, how it works, where it comes from, how to increase its capacity, or change the quality of it… even those who are in the consciousness business disagree, unless they are writing a book together. What is *your* definition? Personally, I like NLP's non-technical, working definition of consciousness: "what we are aware of right now", and everything we are not aware of right now belongs to the domain of unconsciousness… another nice working definition. What we are aware of changes throughout the day, so it is a cumulative phenomenon. NLP gives us a definition of consciousness that we can actually work with. Let's work on what we are aware of right now, and perpetually.

Mihaly Csikszentmihalyi's work suggests there is a cap on how much attention we have access to in a given moment, or even across the span of a lifetime. Our throughput is about 110 bits of information per second, or between 5 and 7 chunks at a time… often less, but seldom more. Agreeing with him, I believe our real task is not to increase our natural conscious capacity, but to direct our limited conscious capacity in ways that bring satisfaction to our self-selected and ecological goals. Want to become a better musician? Adjust what you're paying attention to. Want to have better relationships? Adjust what you're paying attention to. Want to see your bank account fatten up, or your waistline slim down? Adjust what you're paying attention to. Want to see your world more green? You get the picture.

So how can NLP enhance what goes on in consciousness?

NLP starts with the question "what do you want?" From there, NLP sets about restructuring one's cognitive strategies to get that *outcome* in an ecological way, not by doing more of the same, but by doing things differently, and more elegantly. Whether you want to win at work, win in relationships, get closer to God, or support projects to improve the planet, NLP can help you structure or restructure your consciousness to bring these outcomes to pass.

Within the limited light of consciousness, we have other wonderful cognitive resources to help us organize and leverage our limited conscious throughput. Steve Andreas calls these Scope and Categories. Classical NLP would call these aspects *Deletion*, *Distortion*, *Generalization*, or Chunking. Still others would call this Framing and Meta-Framing. For centuries, philosophers have called this the "aboutness" of things… we experience things, then spend huge amounts of time and attention thinking *about* them. By willfully adjusting our scope, categories, chunk sizes, frames, sequences and *submodalities*, our consciousness literally shifts.

NLP reveals the structure of what happens within experience, and then allows us to tweak that structure intentionally in ways that provide better results, without increasing the amount of conscious energy involved. With NLP, we can often get more results with the same or less conscious effort that with the old strategies that were playing out either consciously or unconsciously.

So my definition of raising consciousness is not about recruiting you to support my agendas for how the external world should be. I would rather use NLP to explore your consciousness, and assist you in making your world as rich as it can be for you. In other words, let's tweak the structure of your conscious experience to bring about the outcomes you feel passionate about. Let's use NLP to eliminate those aspects of your strategies that stand in the way of your outcomes, and replace them with better strategies, and watch them play out in the light of your consciousness.

How does NLP compare to meditation?

Meditation focuses one's consciousness on watching the mind, and stops there. NLP also watches the mind, and then tweaks strategies playing in the mind to get a better result. Meditation may ponder problems of the world and hopes for a better one. NLP examines one's interactions in the world, and then consciously adjusts one's interactions to be more inwardly and outwardly congruent. Meditation seeks to treat all things equally. NLP respects similarities and differences, sets outcomes, measures results and makes adjustments along the way to achieve better results. Meditation fosters universal acceptance, NLP fosters acceptance when appropriate, and also exploration and action. If Meditation is a gentle breeze, NLP is a power leaf blower. If Meditation is a deep lake, NLP is a fire hose. If meditation is the diffuse light in all being, NLP is a spotlight where neurological strategies play out and can be altered. Meditation takes one out of the world into the inner world. NLP engages and enhances the inner and outer worlds (in that order).

So I am all for raising consciousness by changing what happens in its light. NLP is a robust and wonderful toolset for doing just this. NLP has tools to help heal the afflicted mind, and stimulate the robust and healthy mind to reach new heights. NLP can help one communicate one's best intentions not only to the universe, but to one's own self, one's family, one's work, or one's community, thereby increasing the odds that the intentions come to fruition.

www.ingramcontent.com/pod-product-compliance
Lightning Source LLC
Chambersburg PA
CBHW042039240426
43667CB00041B/51